MW00635216

Confessions of a Black Conservative

How the Left has Shattered the Dreams of Martin Luther King, Jr., and Black America

By Lloyd Marcus
Unhyphenated American

Confessions of a Black Conservative
How the Left has Shattered the Dreams of Martin Luther King, Jr., and Black America

2009 © Lloyd Marcus
email: mr_lloydmarcus@hotmail.com

Published by: Higher Standard Publishers
www.higherstandardpublishers.com
800-791-5806

ISBN: 978-0-9824027-7-1

All rights reserved. No part of this publication may be reproduced, stored in a retrieval system, or transmitted in any form or by any means-electronic, photocopy, recording, or any other except for brief quotations in printed reviews, without the written permission of the author and/or publisher.

Printed in the United States of America!

Contents

Foreward

I first heard Lloyd Marcus sing at the Gathering of Eagles protest in Washington, D.C. in 2007. He has roused grass-roots conservative activists across the country with powerful songs defending the greatness of our country and spreading the light of freedom.

Lloyd is everything the far Left dreads: A flag-waving, Big Government-spurning, race card-shredding, God-fearing, self-made entrepreneur who grew up in a Baltimore ghetto and refused to stay on the liberal plantation. He refuses to be a "hyphenated America" who puts identity politics above all else. His life story is a story of adversity, adventure, enlightenment, and resilience.

It's a story about choosing personal responsibility over the culture of dependence and blame.

It's a story Hollyweird leftists like Janeane Garofalo don't want you to hear. It's a story that deserves to be told and celebrated.

In Lloyd Marcus, the American Dream is alive and well.

Michelle Malkin
New York Times best-selling author,
blogger, and Fox News contributor

Rev. Dr. Lloyd E. Marcus. and the late Rodelle Marcus

Dedication

Driving home from an Alcoholics Anonymous meeting, I wrote a song to my wife. The hook lyric is, "When I look in your eyes, I can do most anything." Without question, I would not be who I am today had it not been for Christ and His great gift to me, Mary.

Thirty years ago, when she first heard me sing in a nightclub when I sat in with the band, Mary said I should be singing for a living. No one had ever suggested such a thing. When her parents threatened to disown her for dating me, a black man, though extremely painful, Mary said, "So be it. I love him." Over the years, Mary's parents and I have grown to love each other.

When my drinking got out of hand, Mary forced me into rehab and dealt with the financial mess I had created...alone. I've been sober for over twenty years.

When I told her I wanted to risk everything by quitting my successful and financially stable 15 year position as a TV graphic designer to pursue a "pie in the sky" music career, Mary said, "Let's go for it."

I dedicate this book to my amazing and beautiful wife, Mary.

I also honor and dedicate this book to my parents, the late Rodelle Marcus and Rev. Dr. Lloyd E. Marcus.

Special thanks to my Lord and Savior, Jesus Christ.

Coming from the projects, Obama's newly appointed Supreme Court Justice Sonia Sotomayor's story is inspiring. The success of both Obama, a black, and Sotomayor, a Latina, epitomizes the availability of the American Dream to minorities, as well as the greatness of America.

And yet, both harbor resentments and seek to reshape America.

"I would hope that a wise Latina woman, with the richness of her experience, would more often than not reach a better conclusion than a white male who hasn't lived that life." -Supreme Court Justice Sonia Sotomayor

Imagine if a white male nominee made this racist statement in reverse. He would be toast!

Like Sotomayor, I, too, lived in the projects. Allow me to share my story of why I am a proud black conservative.

Introduction

On numerous occasions, I have been asked. "How do we get more blacks to see the light?" In other words, when will blacks stop mindlessly and monolithically voting for liberal democrats who have been promising to fix the same problems in the black community for over forty years. In fact, in areas where loyal black voters have kept liberals in office, problems have gotten worst; epidemically high black male school dropout rates, over 70% black out of wedlock births, black on black crime, etc.

I believe the best way to reach my fellow black Americans is to tell "My Story" which chronicles the virtues of Conservatism in common sense easy to understand non political terms. Conservatism is best for *all* Americans.

Liberals always claim ownership of compassion. In reality, liberalism ultimately hurts people, while true compassion resides and thrives in Conservatism.

In this book, I share life experiences which have convinced me that not only is a conservative approach to life best, it is most nurturing to the human spirit.

You will laugh. You will cry. I pray all readers will be encouraged and my fellow black Americans will see the light and experience true freedom.

America is the greatest land of opportunity on the planet regardless of race, color or creed. One only needs to "Go for it!"

Lloyd Marcus
January 2010

High School Graduation Picture

Chapter 1

Dear White Liberal America

Thank you very, very much. You see us poor, helpless, inferior blacks (forgive me, I must be politically correct, "African- Americans"), and you want to help us using your superior intellect. After all, we could not possibly succeed in this racist, homophobic and greedy country without your assistance.

I first met you guys in the 1970s when I attended the prestigious Maryland Institute College of Art on a scholarship. As a black kid from the ghetto, I found myself among white kids from well-to-do families. I worked a part-time job to cover the cost of my books and art supplies. You guys did not have to work.

And yet, I remember many conversations about how you would never bring a child into this "freaking world" and how "freaking screwed up" this "freaking country... is." You told me how "freaking selfish" your "freaking parents" were, and how they only cared about "freaking money." Then, you drove off in your convertible given to you by your "freaking parents" as I stood at the bus stop.

I cannot thank you enough for the numerous times you shared your expensive premmo weed with me. While I enjoyed the free weed (of which I've long ceased to indulge) and rebellious chicks, in all honesty, I could not figure out what you were so p.o.'ed about.

Now you former hippie boomers are in total control of the government, colleges and public schools, still selling your utopian message of peace and love. Thanks for getting rid of black dads in the home via your welfare programs. I mean, everyone knows dads are cruel chauvinists who beat and molest their kids.

Oh, and thanks for encouraging schools to accept black kids speaking Ebonics rather than English. It would be racist to expect us simple-minded, colored folks to learn to speak English correctly. Besides, we don't want our black kids sounding too white. Authentic blacks must sound like the hood, love rap and Kentucky Fried Chicken. I would never trust any black that eats "sushi" which is probably what those traitors, former Secretary of State Condoleezza Rice and Supreme Court Justice Clarence Thomas, eat. If Justice Thomas would have just answered his phone with a "What up!" and a heartfelt "A-muri-ka sucks," the NAACPC would have championed him as a true brother, faithful to his blackness. Sadly, Rice and "Uncle Thomas," as we call him, chose the character, education and hard work route to success. How disgusting!

Yes, you libs are soooo good to us. I really appreciate "B" actresses like Janeane Garofalo putting that Uncle Tom, RNC Chairman Michael Steele, in his place when she said he suffered from Stockholm Syndrome. How dare he not view himself as a victim of white America. How dare he empower young blacks with the knowledge that they can achieve without liberal intervention. What an ungrateful, well, you know the word I'm thinking. It begins with an "N."

In closing, you libs, please keep up the good work. With your continued diligence, we minorities and most Americans will not have to work or be responsible for anything. Your president is in the process of confiscating the wealth from those greedy rich white S.O.B.s and redistributing it to us. Right on!

Now, if I can just figure out how to tie my shoes all by myself. But if I can't, I know you libs are there for me. Fighting back tears of overwhelming gratitude, again, I thank you.

Lloyd and Hulk Hogan

Chapter 2

ENOUGH with the Race Thing!

Race! Race! Race! As the kids say, "Gag me with Race!" I thought to myself as I read my Republican Senator Mel Martinez's statement on why he was voting to confirm Sonia Sotomayor:

"Given her judicial record, and her testimony this week, it is my determination that Judge Sotomayor is well-qualified to serve as Associate Justice of the United States Supreme Court.

Judge Sotomayor is knowledgeable of the law, would be a fair and impartial judge, and seems to have a good understanding of the limited role the judiciary plays in our democracy.

Judge Sotomayor's rise to the Supreme Court is testimony to the fact that the American dream continues to be attainable. As a Hispanic American, I take great pride in Judge Sotomayor's historic achievement. Given her qualifications and testimony this week, I intend to vote in favor of her confirmation."

Excuse me Mel, but the woman is a leftist who will make decisions based on her "feelings" rather than the law. As a supposed Republican, why the heck would you vote for her? Is it because she is Hispanic? When will we ever get past race in this country?

Voting for Sotomayor simply because she will be the first Hispanic Supreme Court Justice is the same racist reason many voted for Barack Obama. Studies and polls proved that many voters did not have a clue, nor did they care what Obama would do once in office. His black skin color trumped everything. "Let's vote for the handsome, well-spoken black Santa Claus. This will kill two birds with one stone. One, it will prove we are a progressive country. Two, he promises to screw the rich. Cool!"

If only they knew the consequences of their vote.

Annoyingly, even conservatives kept congratulating me on our first black president. I know they meant well, but what I was hearing is "This man is going to destroy our country, but you should be proud, Lloyd, because he is black like you."

While claiming otherwise, Democrats are notorious for making everything about race. Everywhere Democrats go, they immediately count black faces. If the ratio to whites is not high enough, they break out their "racist" rubber stamp.

I remember when the Democrat race exploiters attacked Major League Baseball because not enough blacks were attending the games. Why should MLB be burdened with getting blacks to attend? Are they expected to come up with a racist stereotypical campaign like, "Yo, Ya'll Come!" The Democrats would probably love such a stereotypical campaign as they tend to perceive "authentic" blacks as lovers of rap music and guests on the Maury show having a DNA test to determine the paternity of a child whose mother has slept with twenty men.

I was in the audience at a county grant review hearing. These elderly white veterans were seeking a grant for their museum which displays and restores WWII airplanes. The grant panel chastised them because not enough African-Americans attended their museum. I spoke with several of the veterans afterwards outside. They told me, "We have tried to get African Americans to attend, but they seem uninterested." They even asked me to be on their board. I declined as my plate was pretty full. Yet, it was unsettling to witness these veterans humiliatingly being put on the defensive to counter the panel's implied charge of racism.

I am also president of a nonprofit arts center. A grant required that we list the percentages of every ethnic group we have serviced. I thought, *I cannot do this because we do not keep those kinds of records, nor do we even think of such nonsense. We simply serve our community, red, yellow, black and white, helping working class artists fulfill their creative dreams.* Could you imagine telling a young, brilliant and up and coming artist:

"So sorry, twelve-year-old Sarah. You wrote a wonder-ful song to your terminally ill dad, but we cannot record it because you are white and it would throw off our racial per-centages for this quarter."

We must stop allowing race to trump reason and com-mon sense. The stakes are far too high for the future of America and our children. Do we want our kids living in a world with racial quotas, or a world where all that matters is integrity and excellence in what you do?

Lloyd and Neil Cavuto at a Tea Party in Sacramento, CA

Chapter 3

When Will White America be off the Hook for Sins of the Past?

Oprah, a black woman, is the richest and most influential woman in America and possibly, the world. Michael Jackson's memorial service received unprecedented live coverage by a large number of television networks.

Did I mention that the President of the United States of America is also a black man? With blacks comprising only 13% of the U.S. population, none of these extraordinary black achievements could have happened without tremendous support from white America.

So when will white America be off the hook for sins of the past? When will Democrat pitchmen and women, such as Janeane Garofalo, cease selling the myth that America is a racist country? When will Affirmative Action, which basically says blacks have been screwed in the past, so now it is fair to screw whites, end? When will so-called black leaders, such as Rev. Jeremiah Wright, quit poisoning the minds of blacks with hate and victimhood by preaching that America is controlled by racist rich white people? What else has to happen for the "BIG LIE" to end?

As ridiculous as this sounds, the U.S. Senate, led by Democrats, apologized for slavery. I guess as a black man, this is supposed to make me feel good. The resolution said it was important for Americans to apologize for slavery "so they can move forward and seek reconciliation, justice, and harmony for all people of the United States."

Excuse me, but what the heck have we, as a country, been doing for the past 150 years? America has "moved forward" in every way. This silly, irrelevant apology is all about reparations, more commonly known as "gettin' paid." While the Senate's apology carried a disclaimer that this will not lead to reparations, Democrats are fighting to change that. I am tired of Democrats buying black votes with checks and handouts.

The hideous thing about this scam is that it further sends the message to young blacks that being born black in America comes with "issues"; you're a victim and somebody owes you something. If these politicians truly gave a hoot about young blacks, they would be empowering them with the truth. "You are blessed to be born in the greatest land of opportunity on the planet, America! Education, hard work and doing the right thing will get you wherever you want to be."

I remember when the Star Trek TV series hit the airways. I LOVED the fact that race was not an issue among the multi-racial expert crew. How can we get to that level if the very people who claim to care the most about racial harmony continue playing the "race card" whenever it serves their selfish political purpose?

A very ugly thing is going on in America. Due to a lack of education regarding our history, the Constitution and what has made America great, politicians are extremely success-ful spewing divisive rhetoric that promotes entitlement, victimhood and class envy. "Hate the rich! Hate Whitey! Vote for me! I'll give you their stuff! I'll MAKE them do right by you!" Disgusting. This is NOT my America.

Lloyd at the Veteran's Wall in Washington, DC

Chapter 4

Lloyd Marcus: Black Unhyphenated American!

I traveled on the Tea Party Express tour bus as a singer/ songwriter, entertainer and spokesperson at 34 rallies in 16 states in two weeks. I experienced vicious, racial verbal attacks, but not from the tea party protesters. The racial hate expressed toward me all came from the Left, the very people who support President Obama's radical socialist agenda.

Unfortunately, my deleted email box is littered with numerous messages expressing the following:

"You are the dumbest, self-hating f****** n***** I have ever seen!"

"Maybe this n***** should shut up and learn his place."

How can these be? According to the liberal media, Democrats are saviors, saintly protecting blacks from evil, rich, white conservative Republicans?

These racists are outraged by my opening lines I boldly proclaim at each rally. "Hello, my fellow patriots! I am NOT an African-American! I am Lloyd Marcus, AMERCIAN!"

At every rally, my proclamation inspired great applause, cheers of joy and approval from the audiences. After each rally, many people came to me with tears in their eyes. They said, "I thank you from the bottom of my heart for what you said. I am an Irish (or Italian, or Asian) American. And yet, I would never hyphenate. I feel hyphenating divides us. While it is fine to honor one's origin, let's all be Americans first."

The tea party audience's passionate response to my proclamation was a surprise to me. I did not know so many Americans disapproved of hyphenating pushed on us via political correctness.

I rejected hyphenating years ago. One day I woke up and heard I was no longer black, I was African-American. Anyone rejecting the new term was called ignorant, insensitive and an Uncle Tom if they were black.

I believe most Americans dislike hyphenating. However, enslaved by political correctness and a desire to appear enlightened, sensitive and educated, everyone simply went along with the program.

This hyphenated American thing is like the fairy tale, The Emperor's New Clothes. Con artists convinced the Emperor that the invisible fabric they used for his new attire was so special only the most enlightened could see it. At the public unveiling, the Emperor proudly paraded down the streets in his new outfit while supplicants applauded its great beauty.

Then a little boy yelled, "Mom! Look, the Emperor is NA-KED!" Suddenly everyone, including the Emperor, was forced to acknowledge the truth. Like the little boy in the story who spoke the truth, my public rejection of hyphenating is liberating Americans across the United States. I am inundated with letters of thanks and support.

As I said, I am a singer, songwriter, entertainer and columnist using my gifts to spread the message that conservatism is best for all Americans. The liberals' responses to my YouTube videos, columns and performances on the Tea Party Express have been extremely racist, vicious and hate-filled. In their incredible arrogance, they vilify me for loving my country and not viewing myself as a victim of white America. In the sick minds of liberals, as a black man in America, I must support President Obama regardless of his policies. I must resent white America. I must feel entitled to the earnings of other Americans. My belief, that my success or failure is totally in the hands of myself and my God, is anathema to them.

As to the claim that the tea party protesters are racist, they are not. Quite the opposite. At every rally, with thousands in attendance, I was overwhelmingly showered with affection and thanks for standing up for America. At one rally, a sign read, "Lloyd Marcus for President." These protesters are not racist. They are decent, hard working, ordinary Americans who love their country and disapprove of the radical changes planned by the Obama Administration. Race is not an issue with them. They have deep concerns for their country.

Disgustingly, Obama-ites use race to silence the protesters. They know it is an effective weapon to use against decent people. Ironically, the people the Obam-ites call racist are the same people who hate hyphenating. They want to be united as Americans.

The grand finale of the Tea Party Express Tour took place Saturday, September 12, 2009 in Washington, DC at the U.S. Capitol. I performed my song, "Twenty Ten." The crowd of over a million loved it. C-Span posted my performance on YouTube. Shamefully, C-Span had to delete the hate-filled racist comments posted by Obama supporters in response to my performance. Why do so-called tolerant and compassionate liberals think it is okay to freely use the "N" word when referring to blacks who escape the "liberal plantation?"

Despite the Obama-ite's hideous charges of racism, this amazing tea party movement is driven by passion, concern and love of country by the American people. A Tea Party Express "whistle stop" in Mt. Vernon, Texas epitomized the mood of the movement.

We were late leaving our Dallas, Texas rally and would thus arrive late at our rally in Memphis, Tennessee. The decision was made to cancel the roadside "whistle stop" in Mt. Vernon. It was only supposed to be a brief stop for a few folks to tour the bus, take pictures, and give us homemade treats after all. Soon after, we received a call pleading, "You MUST stop. There are a lot of people here!" The State Police led our Tea Party Express Tour bus into a crowd of 500 to 800 cheering, excited people. They treated us like rock stars. We were totally unprepared. The truck with our sound system was on its way to Memphis, and we did not even have a stage.

We made our way through the crowd to the bed of a pickup truck. National radio talk show host Mark Williams, blue star mom Deborah Johns, singer Diana Nagy, the Rivoli Revue (Ron and Kay) and I climbed on board. Someone handed Mark a bullhorn which he used to encourage the extremely enthusiastic crowd. We recited the "Pledge of Allegiance" and Diana led in the singing of "God Bless America." Many in the crowd were sobbing. They showered us with thanks, hugs, bottled water, bags of snacks and home-made treats. I thought, *How many angry racist mobs bake and bring brownies and overwhelm a black guy with affection and hugs?*

Once back on the bus, our team struggled to hold back tears. We felt humbled, honored and blessed. Though extremely well received at each rally, this "whistle stop" drove home the passion, love of country, and importance of our mission to preserve and take back America!

The mainstream liberal media, ACORN activists, and Obama Kool-Aid drinkers have tried to trash the tea party movement. We've been called "racist, tea bagging rednecks." Critics say the tea parties are the result of marketing by the "vast rightwing conspiracy." Impossible. No marketing firm could inspire such passion in so many so quickly.

Truth be known, this is an incredible grassroots movement driven by love and concern for our great country.

Here are a few of these great American Patriots:

EDNA - Citrus County, FL

Edna in Inverness, FL asked me to sing at her tea party. She borrowed a sound system which arrived 40 minutes before the rally. The need of a CD player for my accompaniment music got lost in communications. The sound guy was a volunteer rather than a sound tech.

An appeal was made to the gathering crowd for a CD player. Three people came forward with CD players, none of which worked for various reasons: improper wires, etc. Someone offered a boom box. We held a mike in front of it. It sounded poorly.

Folks, in the entertainment business this is known as "the gig from hell!" I prayed, "Lord, I don't know what this is about, but I trust You."

Before the arrival of the boom box, I led the crowd, a cappella, in the singing of "God Bless America." When I invited veterans on stage as I sang, "God Bless the USA," it didn't matter that the accompaniment music did not sound good. Emotions, unity and sentiment were high. The crowd of a thousand cheered at the end.

We finally got a CD player and I performed my "American Tea Party Anthem."

Edna is not a professional event planner. She is a patriot committed to serving her country. HER RALLY WAS GREAT!

HEATHER - Santa Barbara, CA

The day before her rally, Heather's sound permit was canceled and her venue chickened out. Her committee had already flown me in from Florida to perform. Heather hung in there, got another permit and a new location. Over 1,200 patriots attended her tea party.

GENE - Lakewood/ Bradenton, FL

Gene booked me to perform at his Florida tea party April 15, 2009. The Tea Party Coalition thought it best for the movement that I perform at the Sacramento, California tea party which would receive national coverage on Fox News and the Neil Cavuto show. Gene graciously agreed.

The tea party protesters are hard working decent people who love their country and want us all united as Americans. I am highly offended that this administration seeks to divide us, not just by race, but also by class envy. As I said to many of the audiences along the Tea Party Express bus tour, "I love you. Stay strong. Do not allow them calling you a racist to shut you up! Stand up for America. God bless you. And God bless America!"

The Star Lloyd Marcus Logo

Chapter 5

Liberals: Wolves in Sheep's Clothing

I still remember the knot in my stomach upon seeing the sea of white faces from the window of our school bus. It was the first day of school in 1961. We came from a neighboring black community, about a hundred or so of us, to the newly integrated white junior/senior high school with thousands of students.

Everything intimidated me: feeling small in the massive school building, being around whites for the first time, wondering if I would measure up to seventh grade schoolwork, and my stutter.

The night before, I shared my fears with my preacher dad. Dad gave his typical answer: "Trust God."

On that first day of school, someone grabbed me from behind. It was an angry, older white teacher with a crew cut. He spun me around and almost pressed his wart-covered nose against mine. In my haste to find my homeroom, I had gone the wrong way on the stairs. Stammering and scared, I tried to explain that I was lost, but he refused to listen and carted me off to the principal's office. There I sat on my first day, a "problem kid," late for homeroom.

Although things did get better, I still felt pretty invisible at Brooklyn Park High in Maryland. The popular black students in the mostly white school were athletically and/or academically gifted. I was neither.

Mr. Gomer, my art teacher and Ms. Hornet, my English/ creative writing teacher, recognized my talents and nurtured them. Every month, the best four art pieces from the entire school were displayed in the lobby. My paintings were selected numerous times. This was not Affirmative Action. My paintings were displayed solely based on merit.

This achievement helped me to realize I had a talent. It dramatically impacted my self-esteem and outlook in life. I won scholarships to attend art college and went on to enjoy an award-winning career as a television graphic designer.

What if my school had embraced a liberal mindset similar to the one so prevalent in public schools today? "EVERY child should experience the feeling of having their artwork displayed in the lobby. It's only fair." If every student's artwork was displayed, it would have robbed me of the knowledge that I possessed above average artistic talent. It would have also given other less artistically talented students a hollow sense of accomplishment and fostered in them a sense of entitlement.

Understanding the fact of life that sometimes you win, sometimes you lose, is paramount to personal growth and development. Without failure, you would never experience the joys of success and fulfillment of achievement.

Conservatism 101: A Tale of Two Dads

Little Johnny hates school and does NOT want to attend. Liberal dad says, "I know how you feel. I hated school also. There are bullies, kids who think they're hot stuff and it is just too HARD! You can sleep as long as you like."

Conservative dad says, "Jonathan Matthew (and his last name) you get your rear end out of that bed this instant and off to school. Why? Because I SAID SO and it is best for your future! And also, because I LOVE YOU!"

Liberals frown upon individual achievement. I heard a news story about a kid banned from Little League pitching because he threw TOO hard. Rather than welcoming an opportunity to raise the game of the batters, liberals chose to force the gifted pitcher to lower his game. Many schools even ban the keeping of score at sporting events. Typical, touchy-feely, let's not cause anyone to feel bad, liberalism.

Folks, I have witnessed the devastating effect of liberalism in my own family. My forty-something, drug-addicted cousin is a serial "impregnator" with several out of wedlock children. And yet, he enjoys a new townhouse, food stamps, free health care and methadone all funded by working taxpayers. In essence, the government is enabling and funding my cousin's irresponsible life-style.

American taxpayers are extremely generous, sympathetic and more than willing to help those in need of a hand up, but liberal cradle- to-grave government dependency programs kill incentive and ultimately hurt people. Meanwhile, Conservatism is branded as mean and heartless.

What is ultimately heartless is an ideology that enslaves people in a system that rewards sloth and discourages achievement. I have witnessed this firsthand as well.

Forever the White Man's Fault

A fierce smell of urine permeated the stairwell of the housing project in which we lived. In the darkness, from smashed light bulbs, the sound of broken wine bottles underfoot echoed off the concrete walls. With the elevators out of service half of the time due to vandalism, many times, I, at the age of nine, was forced to take the scary trek into the shadow of death up the stairwell to our sixth floor apartment located in the projects of East Baltimore.

This housing project was a far cry from the same brand spanking new building we moved into just two years earlier. I fondly remember our excitement when my parents, three younger siblings, and I moved in our apartment. It was a dream come true moving from our leaky-roofed home in the ghetto into a place where everything, including the appliances, was new. We were one of the first families to reside in the eleven-story, all black building. While a few people kept their apartments lovely, most seemed committed to destroying the building.

All I kept hearing from the majority of adults was that everything was the "white man's fault." Even at the tender age of nine, I sarcastically thought to myself, "How can we stop these evil, white people from sneaking in here at night, peeing in the stairwell, leaving broken wine bottles on the ground, smashing the light bulbs, and attacking people?"

My early experience living in the government housing project taught me that some folks simply have a ghetto mind-set. I also witnessed the entrapment of government welfare. Why were so many people angry and violent despite getting free housing, food, and healthcare?

In the late 1950s, my father became one of the first blacks to break the color barrier and become a firefighter with the Baltimore Fire Department. The sight of him in his crisp, blue firefighter uniform made everyone proud, though none more than me. With Dad's new job, the government raised our rent to $72.00 per month. I remember my dad saying, "Seventy-two dollars! They must be crazy. This is too much money! We're movin'!" We relocated to a suburban black community. I truly believe I would not be who I am today had we stayed in the projects.

Several of my cousins remained enslaved to the system and the bigotry of low expectations that government dependency formed in their minds. Because true self-esteem comes from personal achievement, my cousins possessed very little because they achieved very little. They lived angry and bitter lives, consumed with serial impregnating, out of wedlock births and substance abuse. Sadly, an outrageously high number of them died prematurely.

In retrospect, when I hear politicians pandering to the so-called poor of America, it turns my stomach. I've witnessed the deterioration of the human spirit, wasted lives, and suffering that happens when government becomes "Daddy."

How anyone could vote in favor of those who perpetuate such misery is beyond me. Unfortunately, most Black Americans do not realize the "champions" of minorities, i.e. liberals, are the very people responsible for the demise of their communities.

Top Ten Reasons Blacks Should Stop Voting Democrat

10. The same problems Democrats have been promising to fix for forty years have worsened, despite their "efforts."

9. In 1950, 24% of black kids grew up without dads. In 2009, it is now 63%. Seven out of ten black children are born out of wedlock, a result of Democrat encouraged, generational government dependency.

8. The black male high school dropout rate is 40%. Of these dropouts, 72% are jobless and 60% will probably be incarcerated, another consequence of government replacing fathers in the home.

7. Amid the chaos after Hurricane Katrina, Democrat Congressman William Jefferson used the National Guard to return home in order to retrieve $90,000 of suspected bribe

money from his freezer while New Orleans residents were pleading to be rescued from their rooftops.

6. Despite documented proof to the contrary, Democrats tell blacks the same shameful lie that America is racist, and their only hope is to keep electing Democrats to level the playing field.

5. Despite high test scores by inner city black kids in the D.C. school voucher program, Democrats plan to shut it down to appease the teacher unions.

4. Democrats continually seek to lower standards, a glaring example of their bigotry of low expectations of blacks.

3. Most blacks believe marriage should be between a man and a woman. The Democratic Party aggressively supports gay marriage and proposes stronger "hate crime" laws that include protection for pedophiles.

2. The Democratic Party strongly supports abortion on demand, including the murderous partial birth. A disproportionate amount of aborted babies are black. Fifty percent of black babies are aborted. Some call this black genocide (BlackGenocide.org).

And...the number one reason blacks should stop voting Democratic...INSANITY: doing the same thing over and over again, yet expecting a different result!

U.S. Army Training Center, Fort Bragg North Carolina, 1969

Chapter 6

Attitude is
EVERYTHING

I n my youth, I lived a wild and crazy life; drugs, women and partying, basically 24/7. Scholarships permitted me to attend art college where I hung with hippies. While the hippies preached peace and love, most were extremely angry at America.

There I was, a black student from the ghetto of East Baltimore, who could not figure out what these spoiled white kids from well-to-do families were so p.o.'ed about. But, their philosophy was free love and drugs, so I said "Right on!"

I grew weary of my life-style and asked God to help me. He did. I was so excited about my new life, I wanted to share the good news of Jesus Christ with everyone. This led me to join a prison ministry. Talk about a "captive" audience.

I was saddened and stunned by the large number of young black men in prison. Many were bright and gifted in many areas. Yes, they had "issues." Catastrophically, their biggest problem was their negative attitudes and beliefs about

America. Black America's victimhood mindset and negative view of their country are great contributors to their inability to fit comfortably into society. While race profiteers are not totally responsible, I believe we all choose what we want to believe, they have misled many into a belief that limits and hurts them in the long run.

A great example of this occurred to me as a young adult. We were three black boys, gifted artists from the ghetto of Baltimore. I met Dave and Joe, both talented artist/sign painters, when I was hired for the summer at Moe Canale's Sign Shop located downtown across the street from the world famous Lexington Market. My job was silk screen printing signs.

Joe and I were students at the Maryland Institute College of Art. I was a freshman, Joe, a sophomore. Dave rejected college. He was extremely streetwise and thought that college was a waste of time. Dave and Joe learned their sign painting craft at Carver Vo-Tech from their mentor, a black teacher named Mr. Lindy Jordan. They both held Mr. Jordan in high regard.

Our employer, Moe Canale, was a generous, jovial Italian and a good man who treated us well. Moe's personality reminded me of "Fezziwig" in Charles Dickens' *A Christmas Carol*. Whenever a pretty girl passed his sign shop's bay window wearing a mini skirt, Moe would say to us, "Man! Those legs go all the way up." We would all have a good laugh. Hands down, Dave was the most talented in our Three Musketeer band of artists; extremely charming, witty, fun to be around, and always keeping us laughing. Unfortunately, Dave had a dark side. He viewed Moe, our employer, as "the man" or "whitey" and had no qualms about stealing from him. It was the 1970s and many young blacks were militant against America and white people.

On one occasion, Dave stole Moe's coin collection. Surprisingly, Moe forgave him. On another occasion, Dave broke into Moe's desk and wrote himself a check. When Moe found out about it, Dave said he had an emergency and it was only a loan. Moe graciously fired Dave rather than pressing charges against him. As I said, Dave was extremely likable and charming. Remarkably, a few months later, Dave convinced Moe to rehire him.

Joe and Dave were a little older than me. I looked up to Joe like a big brother. My intact family, mother, father and three younger siblings moved out of the Baltimore projects to a black suburban community. Coming to Baltimore to work and attend college was exciting for me.

Joe, like Dave, lived in the ghetto. Joe's dad left when he was five years old Also like Dave, Joe had his juvenile run-ins with the law. At age 16, he spent a year in jail. When Joe returned home, he learned that his mom had suffered a nervous breakdown and was institutionalized. Joe went to live with his grandmother. Today, he thanks his grandmother and Mr. Jordan at Carver High for setting him on the right path.

I admire Joe because he thinks for himself, is a self-starter and a no excuses guy. When we once worked on a college project together, my assignment was to find a special type of paper. I whined to Joe, "I've looked EVERYWHERE and cannot find it!" Joe asked, "Have you looked here? Have you looked there?" I shyly said, "No." "Well then, you have NOT looked everywhere," Joe replied. Although I was annoyed, I knew he was right. That was typical Joe.

After college, I became a graphic designer. I landed a job at an ABC affiliate TV station, and was later promoted to supervisor and enjoyed a successful award-winning career. Joe graduated college, worked his way through graduate school and became the first black art director in a prominent Baltimore advertising agency. He founded a scholarship fund in the names of his grandmother and Lindy Jordan, the black teacher who mentored him. Joe is currently a college professor. We've stayed in touch over the years. A few years ago, I asked Joe about Dave.

Joe said the last time he saw Dave, it broke his heart. Dave was addicted to drugs, mentally diminished and looked like a homeless person. I thought, *Wow, Dave was the MOST gifted of the three of us.*

Life truly is all about choices. Dave thought he knew it all. He was filled with anger and bitterness against an imagined enemy committed to keeping him down. Meanwhile, Joe and I simply pursued our dreams.

Still today, despite the election of America's first black president, "race profiteers" are still selling their "America is racist and whitey is out to get you" rhetoric. Their goal is to birth another generation of entitlement-minded victims seeking reparations. They cannot allow the truth, that America is the land of limitless opportunity for all, to dismantle their lucrative race industry.

Joe and I loved Dave. He was incredibly gifted, fun and exciting to be around. Tragically, Dave chose to embrace the negative entitlement/victimhood rhetoric. In the end, it destroyed him.

I was watching the Glenn Beck show when a black man, Charles V. Payne, founder, CEO and Chief Analyst of Wall Street Strategies was a guest. Payne shared his moving tale of growing up in a poor inner city neighborhood. He said his fellow black students beat him up daily for "speaking too white," getting good grades and daring to have a dream of becoming a businessman. "The kids were not simply jealous of me, they were extremely hostile," said Payne. He attributed the black students' negative attitudes to victimhood and an entitlement mindset instilled in them by liberals.

I thought to myself, *Wow! Black people do not come on TV and tell the truth about the negative effects liberalism has had on the black community. Nor, does anyone hold blacks accountable. Blacks are victims. Each and every problem they could possibly have is the fault of rich, racist, conservative, white Republicans. I mean, everybody knows that!*

I do not remember the details of how I met Fatima, a middle aged black woman dressed in African attire. Fatima was a member of a "back to Africa" group; not physically back to Africa, but rejecting American (slave) names and culture. This intelligent woman was full of rhetoric about the evils of capitalism and white racist America.

Fatima was associated with a supposed national organization. As absurd as this sounds, this black separatist group was demanding the U.S. Government give a state to black America. All blacks who have not succumbed to the seduction of capitalism and remained true to their blackness would gleefully move to this self governing, separate black state.

At that time, I was a young graphic designer employed at an ABC affiliate television station in Baltimore. Fatima approached me to volunteer my graphic design skills for a project benefiting the local black community. I agreed to help. Still, Fatima had an unspoken attitude towards me, "As a brother seduced by 'the man' and 'his system', you owe the black community for your betrayal of your people."

When I delivered my artwork to Fatima's home, there were five young, healthy black men lounging around watching TV. Fatima introduced them as brothers in the revolution eager to move to the soon to be surrendered "black state" where we will finally live with dignity and honor. All of her house guests were unemployed. She had the nerve to ask me to assist her with funds to pay her rent.

I thought, *I'm the guy you think is a sellout traitor to my race by working for the man in his evil capitalist system and you're hittin' me up for money. Meanwhile, you have five bums living in your home contributing nothing whom you highly respect.* I gave her money.

Fatima was a college educated liberal, probably an African-American studies major. She obviously bought into her college professor's anti-American and anticapitalism rants; America is unjust, racist, sexist, greedy and the true source of evil around the world. Her professor's indoctrination infected Fatima with a victimhood and entitlement mental disorder.

Liberals say they are all about "black empowerment" while diminishing blacks' personal power by convincing them that their success is not in their hands, but controlled by evil racist white people and an evil capitalist system. True black empowerment comes from the knowledge that each man's destiny lies in his hands and God.

Recently, I visited Pumphrey, the small suburban black community in Maryland where I grew up. The site of our home, which cost my dad $6,000, was purchased by a young black single mom who grew up in the community. She built an awesome $450,000 home. Pumphrey has several half million dollar homes built by successful blacks who love the community in which they grew up and want to stay.

But how can this be? According to Fatima, Michael Moore, Jeanane Garafolo, Rev. Jeremiah Wright, most Democrat politicians, the liberal media and the Obama administration, minorities are suppressed with little or no opportunity to succeed in America. Remember the words of Rev. Wright, "Barack knows what it is like to live in a culture controlled by rich white people. Hillary ain't never been called a n*****!"

Liberals, both black and white, always relate to blacks like inferior needy, helpless dependents. In their racist arrogance, liberals think an authentic black is "down with rap music," named La-quee-sa, and cannot figure out who's the daddy of her baby after shamelessly sleeping with fifteen men. Sophisticated, educated and self-sufficient blacks are considered out of touch traitors suffering from Stockholm Syndrome.

In Florida, two black women ran for Congress; Republican Jennifer Carroll against incumbent Democrat Corrine Brown. The Brown campaign said Carroll was too articulate, pretty and sophisticated to relate to the poor black constituents in the district. Note that Brown has represented her district for many years with little or no improvements. Brown won. Dr. King surely rolled over in his grave when poverty and ignorance were celebrated while black excellence was considered a campaign negative.

Sadly, most blacks have bought into the leftwing view of America, despite all sorts of evidence to the contrary. I'm on a black liberal professor's email list. The most recent email I received praised Michael Moore, giving his film, *Capitalism: A Love Story* rave reviews.

I am stunned by the passionate "committed to be victims" mindset of the black folks on this list. They act as if blacks are living under the same racist conditions they endured in the fifties.

These blacks are extremely excited and hopeful that their "homey," President Obama, will redistribute the wealth to the poor black community upon whose backs it was earned and unfairly stolen. Even more disturbing is these black liberals are intolerant of the truth. When you confront them with undeniable facts, they resort to calling you names, and threaten physical harm.

Black America's distorted view of their country has contributed greatly to most of its problems: black on black crime, epidemic black male dropout rates, fatherless homes, black genocide via abortion, out of wedlock births and unemployment. Amazingly, the left has convinced blacks that all their problems are the white man's fault, while in reality, all of Black America's problems can be traced back to liberal "blacks are irresponsible idiots and need our help" intervention programs. Without question many liberal programs were not designed with Black America's best interests at heart, but rather to keep them dependent and enslaved to government; thus forever voting for Democrats.

Imagine the impact the left's negative view of America has had on black youths. If America has unfairly stacked the deck against them and whites are burning the midnight oil thinking of ways to keep them down, why should black youths play by the rules? Why study, work hard and do the right thing? Why not join gangs, sell drugs, have babies, get on welfare, steal, etc.?

It is extremely unfortunate that a black "Moses" such as Bill Cosby, Condi Rice, Clarence Thomas or others who have attempted to lead their people to the land of milk and honey--which is America--suffers persecution from power-addicted politicians and arrogant, narcissistic do-gooder liberals.

America is the greatest nation on the planet with limit-less opportunity for all willing to "go for it!" It is cruel, heart-less, irresponsible and evil to tell young blacks otherwise. Black liberals who give Michael Moore rave reviews for his propaganda films trashing America do a great disservice to the Black community. These blacks need to get over their racism and class envy. And yet, they brand us black conser-vatives as Uncle Tom traitors.

Incredible.

Colonial Man & Lloyd Marcus, Tea Party Express 2009

Chapter 7

The Real Race Dividers

I t is truly a sad day in America when the President of the United States fans the flames of racial hatred. The man elected to be president of all the people basically told the NAACP that, although America is racist, sexist and homophobic, you can make it in spite of those white S.O.B.s' attempts to stop you.

"Make no mistake, the pain of discrimination is still felt in America (applause) by African-American women paid less for doing the same work as colleagues of a different color and a different gender; by La-tin-os made to feel unwelcome in their own country; by Muslim Americans viewed with suspicion simply because they kneel down to pray to their god; by gay dead brothers and sisters still taunted, still attacked, still denied their rights."

Are not Obama's statements eerily close to the teachings of Rev. Jeremiah Wright who said, "America is controlled by rich white people"?

How inspiring. The NAACP audience erupted in applause. Obama's condemnation was "red meat" to the liberal organization which is highly protective of its victim status.

Interestingly, Obama's list of victims did not include Christians and straight white males. This is because it is open season on bashing them. According to liberals, everything wrong in the world is the fault of Christians and straight white males. Case in point, a column written in the New York Times by Pulitzer Prize winner Maureen Dowd, demonizes white men.

According to Dowd:

"A wise Latina with the richness of her experiences would more often than not know that a gaggle of white Republican men afraid of extinction would trip her up. After all, these guys have never needed to speak inspirational words to others like them, as Sotomayor has done. They've had codes, handshakes and clubs to do that..."

Mr. President, one of those African-American women you claim America has victimized used her money, power and influence to help get you elected. White guys did not blow up the Twin Towers murdering over three thousand Americans. Muslims did. So, excuse me if I give them a second glance in an airport. Only illegal Latinos are unwelcome, just as with every other ethnic group, and when an openly gay beauty pageant judge viciously trashes a contestant for humbly saying she believes marriage should be between a man and a woman, and much of the media sides with him in ridiculing the woman, it is safe to say America is pretty tolerant of homosexuals.

All of Obama's accusations against America are untrue, divisive and evil. Does racism exist in America? Of course it does, along with every other sin. Are we a racist country? Absolutely not! Why would our president want to reinforce such a divisive paradigm? And why did the NAACP so enjoy Obama's attack on white America?

If Dr. King were magically brought back to life, he would be heartbroken over what has become of this organization and the civil rights movement. He would ask, "Is Jesse still running to every photo op? And, tell me again how did this Reverend Al guy become our spokesperson"?

Dr. King required his marchers to be sober, neat, clean and even tempered. He never preached hate. Quite the opposite, Dr. King dreamed of a day when all of God's children, black and white, would join hands as brothers and sisters. Dr. King fought, suffered and died because he wanted the Negro (and that is a word he proudly used) to have an equal opportunity to strive and achieve excellence.

Dr. King would beam with pride over former Secretary of State Condoleezza Rice and U.S. Supreme Court Justice Clarence Thomas, both hated by the NAACP. I can hear him saying, "Negroes, Secretary of State and U.S. Supreme Court Justice, praise God!"

Dr. King's once great organization has become a liberal partner with the Democratic Party in their exploitation of blacks. Keep telling them they are victims, America is against them, and they will continue to need Democrats to defend and protect them. This will ensure that the NAACP will remain relevant and Democrats will continue getting 95% of the black vote. This is exactly why the NAACP went wild with applause over Obama's speech trashing America.

If MLK were alive today, I believe he would be a proud member, not of the NAACP, but of the organization of which I am President, the National Association for the Advancement of Conservative People of Color.

The NAACP's philosophy and goal is far more in keeping with Dr. King's dream: personal responsibility, judging people by the content of their character rather than the color of their skin, and the belief that America is the greatest land of opportunity on the planet for all people. On the contrary, our president believes she is an evil place where successful white males victimize everyone. Dr. King would be appalled.

I am tired of the left being allowed to make the rules regarding race. Imagine the absurdity of a competition in which one side is allowed to set the rules against their opponent. The left tells us what is racist. The left tells us what we can and cannot say. The left published a cartoon depicting former black Secretary of State Condolezza Rice as an Aunt Jemimah; another depicted Rice as a huge-lipped parrot for her "massa": Bush. Neither illustrations were considered racist by their creators or publishers, or even widely condemned by the left.

In opposition to black Republican Michael Steele's campaign to run for U.S. Senate, a liberal blogger posted a doctored photo of Steele with a black face and big red lips, made to look like a minstrel. The caption read, "Simple Sambo wants to move to the big house." Not one Democrat denounced these racist portrayals of black conservatives.

And yet, a sign seen at a tea party depicting Obama as a witch doctor is considered by the left to be beyond the pale and obviously racist. Why is the left, given their track record of bias, granted final authority to determine the intent of the sign? Why do we conservatives so quickly and easily allow ourselves to be put on the defensive?

The rules set by the left are extremely clear: racist images of black conservatives and negative images of Bush are fair game. Even a play about murdering President Bush was called "harmless art." Meanwhile, all unflattering images of Obama are racist, and constitute dangerous, potentially violent hate speech.

New York Times columnist Maureen Dowd called Congressman Joe Wilson a racist for saying, "You lie" to President Obama. Using her psychic powers, Dowd said Wilson was really saying in his mind, "You lie, BOY!" Yet when liberal commentator Julianne Malveaux said she hopes black conservative Supreme Court Justice Clarence Thomas' wife "feeds him a lot of fatty foods so he will die early from heart disease like many black men," it was not considered racist.

I am a black conservative singer, songwriter, entertainer and columnist. Liberals have posted comments all over YouTube and C-SPAN freely using and calling me the "N" word. Because they are liberals and I am considered an uppity, off the liberal plantation, runaway black, all tactics to restore me to my owners are acceptable.

Nothing could be a clearer example of playing the race card to squelch dissent than the treatment of Rush Limbaugh. I have been a faithful Rush Limbaugh radio show listener for almost 20 years. I have never heard Rush make one racist comment. As a matter of fact, I am a black man who has been inspired and encouraged by Rush on numerous occasions.

Rush was part of a partnership bidding to purchase an NFL football team. I was highly offended watching the liberal media's all out assault on this great American. In their efforts to block Rush from ownership of a team, the liberal media and the left attempted to brand Rush as a racist.

The media's charges of racism against Rush were completely based on supposed "racist quotes" which cannot be documented and comments knowingly taken out of context from his radio show. As a member of Rush's weekly 20 million listening audience, I took the assault on him personally. If Rush is a racist, then isn't it logical to assume that we, his listeners, are equally guilty for tolerating his racism?

Obviously, Rush's accusers have never listened to his radio show or else they simply have an agenda. It is truly disheartening and infuriating to witness the media's frenzied character assassination of Rush built on falsehoods and hearsay without one shred of evidence. Knowing the truth about Rush, how can I possibly trust any reporting by the mainstream media?

Adding insult to injury, Rev. Al Sharpton, considered to be a respected spokesperson for the black community by the liberal media, weighed in with his opposition to Rush being allowed to own a team. Given Sharpton's role in the Tawana Brawley scam, it is truly amazing that he is considered a credible representative of the black community...talk about Bizarro World. How dare this characterless conman pass judgment on Rush!

Beyond Rush, the larger issue is the tyrannous yoke political correctness has on our society and the swift punishment delivered with an iron fist by its enforcers, the liberal media. Rush's true crime is boldly speaking the truth about several of the liberal media's sacred cows, challenging their premises and opposing their far left agenda.

As I stated before, the NAACP, a sacred cow of the left, is without question a liberal partisan organization. Rush, a white guy, stated this truth out loud, thus violating rule number one on the media's politically correct list of do's and don'ts. "Whites under no circumstances are permitted to publicly criticize blacks."

Offenders are verbally flogged within an inch of their lives and branded with a virtual "R" for "racist" on their forehead.

While I stand beside my hero, Rush Limbaugh, there is a much larger issue at stake extremely threatening to our freedom, liberty and culture. We cannot trust the mainstream media. We are at war; liberal media's and the left's political correctness versus the freedom and free speech of the America people. Our enemy's mission is to silence all dissent. We serfs must worship their sacred cows or suffer the consequences.

The liberal media and the left have been attempting to silence Rush and other conservatives for years. Make no mistake about it, their latest bogus "Rush is a racist" campaign is another stealth attack on our freedom of speech. It is extremely important that lovers of freedom rally around Rush Limbaugh. Silencing Rush would be a major victory in their quest to silence and control us all.

Another example of the left setting the rules is the tea party movement. "Take Back America!," a common tea party rallying cry, is now deemed racist. Again using their psychic powers, the left claims the protesters are really saying, "Because the president is black, let's take America back"! This is totally absurd. "Take Back America" refers to the hijacking of our freedoms, liberty and culture by an out of control administration.

I was asked to perform at a tea party event. The organizer informed me, "I want to get away from calling the rally a 'Tea Party' because the liberal media have made the term negative." I said, "Does this mean you do not want me to sing my American Tea Party Anthem? Then, why am I here?" Politeness to my host prevented me from saying, "News flash, pal! The media is going to trash us regardless of what we call our rallies. It's what they do. They are not on our side. Should we keep changing what we call the rallies in hope of finding a name which will cause the media to give us fair coverage?" A million people showed up in Washington, DC for the September 12th Taxpayers Rally. The media reported 70,000.

I was interviewed on CNN. During the phone pre-interview, the young black producer asked me, "Is there any part of Obama's health care plan you like?" I replied, "No." He was stunned. With great shock and disbelief in his voice, the producer repeated my reply with a loud "NO?" He then abruptly said, "I'll call you back." News1News posted my CNN interview on YouTube with the following caption, "African American Right Wing (Obama Hating) Singing Tea Bagger, Lloyd Marcus." Folks, I am a Christian and hate no one, but this is what the media does to those who disagree with them. All who oppose Obama's agenda are considered racists, rednecks or just plain stupid.

The stakes are far too high to allow the left to continue setting the rules of engagement. The far left and Obama administration have a vision for America that is very different from our Constitution. As patriots, it is our duty to just say, "NO!"

My black 82-year-old dad told me he has seen the reports on TV on how a lot of people at the rallies want Obama dead. I said, "I bet you saw that on CNN." Dad said, "Yes." It infuriates me that CNN is selling the lie that the Tea Party Movement is all about racism and hatred for a black president. While my dad has never said anything out loud, I thought, *What must he think of me? Why is his firstborn siding with these evil white folks against a fine fellow black man?* I replied, "Dad, try watching FOX."

An Open Letter to Jeanane Garafalo

Ms. Garafalo,

HOW DARE YOU call hard working, decent American taxpayers "racist tea bagging rednecks" simply because they protest outrageous government spending! Your irresponsible divisive accusation fuels the flames of racial hatred and could inspire violence against whites.

Your arrogance in saying that I suffer from "Stockholm Syndrome" because I am a black man who loves his country and his fellow Americans is beyond measure.

I cannot begin to express how offensive it is for me to hear narcissistic, superior liberals lecturing me on why I should view myself as a victim and hate white America. You are sick, evil or both.

As a black man, I ask that you please confine your liberal insulting rhetoric on my behalf to your elitist cocktail parties where you pat yourselves on the back for the number of blacks on your guest list.

The American people are good. Obama was elected president, NOT king. We have a right and duty to protest against policies we believe to be wrong for America. Why? Because freedom isn't free!

Your despicable lies only embolden us patriots to stand tall, united and strong for America.

Lloyd Marcus

Ron, Dianna, Kay, Lloyd on The Tea Party Express

Chapter 8

The Real Cure for Racial Harmony: Seeing People as Individuals

Some people are screwed up. Broken. They choose to hate and nothing will change their minds. I believe most people are basically good. Given an opportunity, they work things out.

In 1956, my dad, Rev. Lloyd Marcus Sr., was one of the first blacks to break the color barrier into the Baltimore City Fire Department at Engine 6. Unlike the white firefighters, Dad did not have free reign of the firehouse. A bunk, toilet, sink and single set of eating utensils were marked "reserved" for him. Even the general coffee pot was off limits. When white firefighters voted on which TV program to watch, Dad was excluded.

The other firefighters refused to speak to Dad, except to criticize or chastise him for a rookie mistake. His pleasant "Good Morning" and "Good Evening" were met with cold stares and silence. Sometimes their disdain got to Dad. Feeling obligated as a representative of Christ, he remained pleasant.

Dad was also a young assistant pastor at a storefront church. Optimistic by nature, he found a blessing in the white firefighters' rejection. Dad said it caused him to spend a lot of time praying and studying his Bible in the back storage room, which they sarcastically called "the pastor's office."

On one occasion, Dad could not find the spoon marked "reserved" to stir his cup of instant coffee. He put another spoon in his cup and went to get some milk. Upon his return, Herman, a white firefighter had the spoon in his hand. "This is one of our spoons. You keep your filthy hands off of it!" Herman threw the spoon into the sink, turned and walked away. Dad said he took his Bible to the back storage room and prayed, "Lord, give him to me."

Herman and Dad had another run in. Like the whites, Dad had propped his foot on a wooden chair while shining his shoes. When Herman ordered Dad to get his foot off of the chair, Dad said he was not harming the chair. Angered, Herman yelled at Dad, "If you don't get your foot off of that chair, I'm going to punch you in your black nose!"

That was the last straw! Despite knowing he could be terminated with five kids and a wife to feed, testosterone trumped reason that day. Dad challenged Herman to "duke it out" outside after their shift. The shift officer caught wind of their scheduled duel and ordered Dad to go home immediately after his shift.

Two years had passed when a new white firefighter came upstairs to Dad's bunk and invited him to join them for a cup of coffee. Dad accepted. Amidst grumbling from other white firefighters, Dad drank his first cup of coffee from the general coffee pot.

Dad stayed with the department committed to excellence in his work and remaining pleasant.

About four years into Dad's career, Engine 6 responded to a fire in a two story building. The shift officer ordered his men out of the blinding, smoke-filled inferno. A firefighter named John asked, "Where's Marcus?" John immediately ran back up the ladder and into the deadly smoke and flames. Herman, who once threatened to punch Dad in his black nose, was right on John's heels.

Dad's mask had malfunctioned. He became overcome by smoke and disoriented. A thought came to him, *Everyone has to go sometime. You're going to die by fire.* Dad instantly said, "Jesus! Jesus!" Then, the floor turned upside down as he passed out. Dad awoke to someone calling his name, "Marcus! Marcus! Marcus!"

Dad yelled, "Over here!" John saw the light from Dad's flashlight and crawled towards the light. He dragged Dad to the window where he and Herman carried him down the ladder. Dad said he remembers Herman's comforting voice,

"Hang in there Marcus. You're okay. We got you...we got you!"

The hospital staff had to open windows because the smoke in Dad's clothes and skin burned their eyes. Miraculously, Dad was not burned and made a full recovery. Dad went on to win Firefighter of the Year two times.

Herman, John and Dad became great friends. John was a licensed plumber on the side. On one occasion when our pipes froze, John repaired them in freezing weather in the crawl space under our home for free. Dad, now in his eighties, was honored to speak at both Herman and John's funerals.

What changed the hearts of these white men causing them to risk their lives to save the life of a black man? I do not know. However, I suspect it had something to do with Dad's character.

Lady Liberty

We all hear the generalizations, "White people are this! Black people are that!" In reality, people are simply individuals.

Herman, John and my Dad were three decent men with various upbringings and beliefs who found common ground and friendship. God did answer Dad's prayer. He gave Dad Herman and threw in John for good measure.

Chapter 9

Obama's Attack on Achievers and Individual Rights

R ecently, I thought of two Hall of Fame base ball players, Baltimore Orioles Frank Robinson and Cal Ripken Jr. On several occasions, I witnessed Robinson, at the bottom of the ninth with two outs, dramatically hit the game winning home run. Most players may hit the game winner once in their careers. Incredibly, Frank Robinson hit the "big one" numerous times.

Cal Ripken Jr. holds the record for going 2,632 games without missing a single day at work. Loved for more than his dependability, he was a quiet player beaming with character. When Cal announced his retirement, there was much fanfare and worldwide media attention surrounding his final game. Astonishingly, Cal hit two home runs at that final game. The crowd and both teams cheered wildly for him. Extremely moved, Cal spontaneously jogged around the stadium and the crowd went nuts. Had this perfect scenario happened in a movie, people would have said it was too corny to be real. It was a truly wonderful, moving and inspiring moment. One so moving, I wrote a tribute to Ripken's achievements entitled, "Ironman."

Watching these events I wondered, what is it that makes a person do the impossible repeatedly at the perfect moment? Something special must tick within Michael Jordan, Bruce Lee and other highly successful individuals.

The common thread that ties these high achievers together is character and strong work ethic, and it leads to pure EXCELLENCE.

Here in America, we are blessed with the precious gift of freedom. While freedom does not guarantee equal outcomes, it does give one a rare opportunity to rise to the pinnacle. In most countries, if your parents are peasants, you are guaranteed the same fate. In America, opportunities are limitless, restricted only by one's sheer will to GO FOR IT! There is something wonderful and American about striving to be the BEST, competing, winning (and losing), and exemplifying good character and hard work.

Horrifically, the Obama administration is committed to reshaping America. Using "class envy" which appeals to our lower nature, Obama has successfully demonized achievers. He accuses them of being greedy and selfish. The supposed "Great Unifier" has no qualms using his bully pulpit to divide Americans by proclaiming, "You have too little because THEY have too much." His "spread the wealth around" agenda is in direct opposition to the roots of American exceptionalism.

Ponder this for a moment folks. Like no president before him, President Obama traveled around the world on his "America is Too Successful and Arrogant Apology Tour." WOW!

My mom was a domestic worker. She cleaned white folk's homes and did ironing. She was respected for her honesty and character. My dad was one of the first blacks who broke the color barrier into the Baltimore City Fire Department. Despite horrendous treatment by the white firefighters, my dad won "Firefighter of the Year" TWO TIMES! Neither of my parents EVER taught my four younger siblings and me that we were ENTITLED to the earnings of others. My parents, by example, taught us the joy, dignity and pride of a job well done and earning our own money. My dad has been working since the age of 12, when he was the delivery boy for a fish merchant. As the fish cart rolled through the neighborhood, customers would yell their orders from their window. After the fish man cleaned and wrapped the order, Dad would run the fish to the customer. Dad said he earned $1.25 for the day. Out of his earnings, Dad assisted his aunt who raised him, purchased a sports shirt for 45 cents, treated himself to a movie and still had money for snacks. Dad recalled bragging to his buddies, "Man, I'm buying my own clothes now."

The young entrepreneur also shined shoes at the Greyhound bus terminal on Saturday nights from midnight to 8 am the next morning, earning 10 cents a shine plus tips. Dad quickly learned tips were bigger when he added a little show-manship, such as popping the cloth and twirling the brushes. Dad said, "It's all in the presentation. Most Sunday mornings, I went home with as much as $5." As he told me the story at eighty years old over the phone, I could still feel the pride and joy in Dad's voice.

My mom also worked as a custodian at the high school. Though she was extremely intelligent, mom's crazy dysfunctional upbringing left her with emotional issues.

Mom's childhood was a nightmare. I'm a baby boomer born after the war. My generation was blessed with the opportunity to choose what we wanted to do with our lives. Mom's life had been consumed with survival. Dreaming of a desired future appeared arrogant to her.

As much as I know Mom loved me, I always felt a little resentment that life offered me so many more choices than her. A gifted artist, I was able to attend college and become a professional artist.

In the 40s, Mom's big dream was to work as a sales clerk in one of the classy downtown Baltimore department stores. I still remember the pain and sadness in Mom's eyes when she told me that upon filling out the application, they immediately directed her to the kitchen. Mom believes it was because of her dark complexion.

Mom's emotions were quite complicated. She could be loud and quick to anger, yet extremely compassionate with a huge heart for the underdog. Mom was also a romantic. She loved the *I Love Lucy* television show. I felt Lucy's antics reminded mom of herself. I remember watching her cry while watching the episode where Lucy was having a difficult time finding the right moment to tell Ricky she was "having a baby." They couldn't say pregnant on TV at that time. She was devastated when Lucille Ball and Desi Arnaz divorced.

First born of five, I believe I inherited Mom's emotionalism and compassion. Sometimes I overconnect with the pain of others. I struggle to keep a balance. Profound truth, honor and love also cause me to tear up always leaving me feeling embarrassed.

Mom worked as a domestic for much of her life. When we were kids, white ladies would come to our home to pick up ironing Mom did for them. From my twelve-year-old point of view, I felt Mom's white employers liked and respected her.

As a kid in elementary school, Mom's unusual name embarrassed me. It was Rodelle. Though she never had opportunity to explore her full potential, she possessed many talents. She was a gifted cook and baker. Her handwriting was beautiful. She was a fast learner.

When Dad applied for the Baltimore Fire department, Mom assumed the role of his drill instructor. The department had a system of long and short bell rings to alert firefighters of different situations. Mom learned the system instantly. She tapped a spoon against a drinking glass to simulate the bells, and then would say to my dad, "No stupid, that's wrong! Now, listen this time!" In her tough loving way, she taught Dad the system.

Dad enrolled in Bible college while working fifteen hour night shifts for the fire department. Mom edited and hand-wrote his essays for school. She studied and prepared him for tests. She and Dad joked that his degree belonged to both of them.

Over time, Mom grew progressively comfortable in her role as a pastor's wife. However, ghosts from her troubled childhood materialized on occasion causing her to feel inferior, fearful and insecure. Long after the ritzy downtown restaurants integrated, Mom still never felt comfortable dining in the mostly white establishments.

Her fearful overly cautious approach to life frustrated me as a child. "Don't play sports because you may get hurt. Don't audition for anything because you may embarrass yourself." Thank God Dad was around to counter her paranoia.

Even after we five kids grew up and moved away, Mom still kept her refrigerator and freezer full. She was all too familiar with hunger was a child. Food symbolized security to Mom. Typical of her mindset, Mom struggled with being overweight for as far back as I can remember.

I suspect my conversations with Mom only scratched the surface of her childhood suffering. I sensed that some things were just too painful or embarrassing of which to speak. It saddens me that Mom viewed much of her life as something to get through, avoiding harm rather than to be enjoyed.

Mom just wanted to feel safe, have a roof over her head and food in the fridge. After 45 years of marriage to my Dad, Mom lost her battle with diabetes and passed away.

Regretfully, many Americans today feel entitled to the earnings of others. Such a concept was never in my parents' realm of thinking. In their minds, you simply do the right thing, work hard and reap the rewards of a job well done. By the way, like my dad, I began working at age 12 for a neighbor. And also like my dad, I took pride in doing a good job and making my own money.

If one works harder, is smarter and invests more wisely than others, why shouldn't he/she reap the benefits? Does stealing from the rich make you a winner or a loser? I'm sorry, but people who are consumed with "class envy" and "entitlement" are losers. The Good Book says, "Thou shall not covet." Winners celebrate excellence and strive to emulate it.

Obama wants a nation of losers. He seeks to reward failure, laziness and bad behavior, while punishing achievers to facilitate his massive power grab and devastating intrusion on our freedom. Outrageously, he fired the CEO of General Motors. Now, he wants to 'cap' salaries. This is TOTALLY un-American. When did we vote to change the Constitution giving government control over private sector businesses?

Everyone is concerned about the spread of the H1N1 virus. I pray that the "entitlement mindset" bug, spread by Democrats and Obama, does not infect too many Americans. The day most Americans believe they are ENTITLED is the day we die as a great nation.

My fellow Americans, we MUST preserve and defend the RIGHTS and FREEDOM of the INDIVIDUAL!

Chapter 10

You Racist!

ObamaCare: A Case Study on Disagreeing with Obama

I am on the email list of a dear black friend of 20 years. He is a minister, writer and professor. He has mentored and advised me with great wisdom on numerous occasions. With me being a black conservative Republican and he a Democrat, we avoid talking politics. Since the election of Obama, my friend will talk about nothing else. He is in Baltimore. I'm in Florida. Every time he calls me, he turns the conversation into trashing all who oppose Obama's agenda. Thank God for caller ID.

I received a mass email from my friend in which he vilifies the Christian community for not chastising ministers who speak against Obama and for not attacking Sarah Palin. He said the Republicans used Palin as their "attack dog against Obama." He said watching a McCain/Palin rally was like watching a KKK lynch mob and he personally heard the crowds yelling "kill him!" referring to Obama. Folks, my dear friend is a liar.

In 2008, I traveled throughout the U.S. attending forty rallies on the national "Stop Obama Tour" with Our Country Deserves Better PAC. Not once did I hear any violent or racist comments. Seeing through his smooth speeches and charisma, people were simply terrified of what was to come with an Obama victory, especially with regards to health care.

Behind all of my friend's intellectual yada, yada, yada, festers a deep hatred for the rich and white people. In one conversation, he said with great glee that Obama was going to "rein in Wall Street" and CEO salaries should be limited to $500,000 per year. I thought, *Who the heck are you to dictate how much someone should be permitted to earn? This is America. The sky's the limit.*

Anger caused me to write a passionate reply to my friend's hate filled email. I stated numerous reasons why Obama's agenda and the health care bills are wrong for America.

Included was abortion. Fifty percent of black babies in America are aborted. (BlackGenocide.org) Obama voted three times against protecting babies who survive an abortion. How does my black minister friend justify supporting Obama. And why does he consider anyone opposing Obama's policies non Christian, racist or an Uncle Tom if you are black?

Ready to hit "reply all" I remembered the White House request that all emails against ObamaCare be forwarded to them. I thought, why give them more ammo to attempt to shut me up? The folks on my friend's liberal email list are all infected with Obama Brainlock Syndrome. They do not want to know the truth. In the current climate set by our "I'm gonna make you a health care offer you can't refuse" president, I could be setting myself up for physical attacks.

Along with their determination to force ObamaCare down our throats, there are two other extremely disturbing aspects of the Democrat, Obama administration and liberal media's behavior. One, they will do or say whatever necessary to win. Two, they don't give a hoot about the will of the American people.

Speaker of the House Nancy Pelosi said at the town hall meetings she saw people wearing swastikas, which no one else saw, implying that the frustrated constituents were a bunch of racist Nazis. Senate majority leader Harry Reid accused the town hall attendees, mostly seniors, who were offended being lied to by their representative as being an "angry mob." The liberal media, the third arm of the Obama hit squad, faithfully did their part. Out of the thousands of signs at the town hall meetings and tea parties, CNN and other liberal media focused on one sign of Obama dressed as a witch doctor. CNN especially aired the Obama witch doctor sign over and over and over again. They accompanied the video of the sign with their liberal bias commentators excoriating the tea parties as nothing more than racist hate filled gatherings. All three, Pelosi, Reid and the liberal media, without thought of consequence, or even considering the destruction of race relations in our country, recklessly play the race card calling all who oppose Obama Care racist. This is totally irresponsible.

The American people are not stupid. They sense Obama's deception and they can read. The American people know ObamaCare equals massive government infringement on our freedom, rationed health care, funding for numerous liberal extremist programs and a debt our great, great, great grandkids will be burdened with paying. And yet, Democrats and the President, displaying incredible arrogance tell us we are wrong. I say, Democrats and Mr. Obama, "You lie!"

It's an old comedy skit. Wife comes home catching her husband in bed with another woman. The wife is livid screaming at the couple. They calmly get out of bed, get dressed, make the bed and the woman leaves. The husband says, "What woman? What are you talking about?" The adulterous husband then walks out of the bedroom. The wife stands there puzzled questioning her sanity.

Obama is attempting to pull this same trick on the American people regarding his health care bill. Town hall meeting attendees across America have read the bill and are expressing outrage over various items. Displaying incredible arrogance, lack of character and "hutzba," Obama says, "this and that is not in there...you're all parroting absurd vicious rumors spread by racists and Republicans."

Still believing in the power of his persona as the "Good Shepherd," Obama thinks he can simply wave his mighty staff and say. "Just trust me regarding your heath care" and like sheep, the American people will follow. But how can we possibly surrender something as important as the health of our families on the word of a man who has displayed such glaring absences of character?

During the Clinton presidency, the liberals successfully sold many Americans the concept that "character doesn't matter."

Well, folks, the liberals are wrong. Character always matters, especially in the highest office in the land. A difficult and painful experience taught me that my character and my word are extremely valuable. Your character and your word define you.

In 1993, callers to the Rush Limbaugh radio show said they were "let go" due to company downsizing. Rush encouraged them to view their layoff as an opportunity to pursue their dreams. Inspired by Rush and with permission from my amazing wife, I resigned from my 15-year position as an award winning graphic designer and supervisor at an ABC affiliate TV station. I wanted to pursue my life long dream of becoming a recording artist and entertainer. It never dawned on me to have a game plan. I simply quit.

Upon arriving home, Mary informed me that she had paid all the bills and we had eight dollars in the bank. I am grateful that God takes care of idiots. Through a series of miracles, we survived. Still, we went from annually hosting "Lloyd and Mary's Island Party" for 200 guests, which was always covered in the Baltimore society pages to extreme poverty. After three years, I was offered a position with an entertainment company based in Orlando, FL. It required that we relocate from Maryland. At that time, we were driving a late eighties Lincoln purchased from dear friends. Before the sale, they informed us that the car had a minor oil leak which their mechanic said could be fixed for a few hundred dollars. It was the oil leak from hell. Despite taking the car to a major chain and charging $1,500 on our credit card, the oil leak grew worse. Frustrated and angry, Mary and I feared the Lincoln would not make the 1,200 mile trip to Florida. We must dump-excuse me-sell the car. Our newspaper ad drew no response.

Meanwhile, we had sold our home and the dates were fast approaching for us to vacate the house and arrive in Florida. Pressure was mounting. Finally, an old man inquired about the Lincoln. Mary scheduled a meeting at a fast food restaurant. If he liked the car, she would follow him home to make the transaction. Desperate to sell, I wanted nothing to go wrong. I heard men like women wearing bright colors so I told my beautiful blonde wife to wear her red dress.

The old man was white. We are a black/white interracial couple and I did not want anything to "blow the deal." I thought it best that I not be seen and simply followed Mary in our second old car. Mary's meeting with the old man went great. He enjoyed their chat and the Lincoln. He asked Mary to follow him home to finalize the transaction. I followed a safe distance away. When we reached his home-this was prior to the era of cell phones-I tried to telepathically tell Mary not to park in his driveway! He would surely see the oil leak. She parked in the driveway.

Mary stayed in his home for what seemed like forever. The old man was pretty frail and non-threatening so I had no reason to fear for her safety.

Finally, Mary came out and got in the car with $3,000. We gave each other an excited high five hand slap. She said the man was lonely and really liked her. She also liked him. The old man was thrilled to have someone view his family albums and listen to his stories. His wife, the love of his life, was in a nursing home. He visited her every day. Despite Mary's compassion and admiration of his love for his wife, we were consumed with tunnel vision to dump the "thorn in our sides."

I rationalized, "The man is in his late eighties. He only drives to the nursing home. The oil leak is no big deal for him."

We lived a few hours away. Upon arriving home, the phone rang. It was the old man. *Mr. Marcus, that car is leaking oil something fierce. Can I get my money back?*

Suddenly, I awoke from my fog of deceit. A horrible feeling of shame and embarrassment came over me. Just as Judas had sold his soul for thirty pieces of silver by betraying Christ, I sold my character for $3,000. Enthusiastically I said, "YES SIR, we will return your money." Apparently, Mary had come to her senses as well. She, too, felt that we must return his money.

This incident happened on a Friday. Commitments forced us to put off visiting the old man until Monday. I was sick with guilt and shame all weekend. I could not touch that money. Life had given me a squeeze and I was devastated by what came out of me. Mary and I were so happy when we returned his money. Remarkably, the old man kept applauding us for being such great people.

Whether teachers, clergy, politicians, handymen or anyone we allow into our lives, character always matters. No, Mr. Obama, we cannot simply just "trust" you regarding our health care.

Many sincere white Americans thought that by electing a black president, America could never again be characterized as a "racist country." Shamefully, this characterless administration betrayed Obama voters by exploiting race, using it as a tool to implement their far left agenda, such as health care. If you don't agree with everything Obama wants, you must be a racist. Rather than the election of America's first black president bringing unity among different ethnicities, Obama's administration is tearing us apart. They will continue to play the tired, old, and tattered geriatric "race card" as long as it is effective.

Folks, PLEASE do not fall for it. The stakes are far too high. Boldly speak the truth and stand up for what you know in your hearts to be right for America. Obama wants to redistribute wealth, punish achievers, decide who lives or dies and control as much of our lives as possible. It is just that simple. His agenda must be stopped. Do not allow yourself to be manipulated and intimidated by the fear of being called "racist."

Ironically, "Black Racism" has blinded my long time friend as well as many other black Americans from seeing beyond Obama's skin color. Dr. King would not be proud.

Lloyd in the recording studio next to Bill Scott
Frank Starch, producer, far right

Chapter 11

Democratic Policy: Throw Americans Under the Bus

When President Obama nominated Sonia Sotomayor for the Supreme Court, he said she was selected because he wanted someone who would show "empathy." It occurred to me at the time that Obama wants the same behavior from America's police force.

Professor Henry Lewis Gates Jr. was arrested for disorderly conduct. Because Gates is black, the White House launched a race committee to "teach" police to be more sensitive. Like his Supreme Court nominee, Obama wants police to give special consideration to race when enforcing the law. In other words, before you white cops arrest a black person for a crime, think of America's original sin of slavery and all that liberals say blacks are still going through. Perhaps an "I understand where you're comin' from bro" before you cuff him.

Obama's race committee is an absurd waste of taxpayers' money. What on earth does arresting someone for disorderly conduct have to do with race? Gates is either guilty or not guilty. His skin color is irrelevant. Obama making Gates' arrest about "race" is extremely telling; an insight into his belief about white police.

Even though Obama retreated from his original "the police acted stupidly" statement, he still implied that the white arresting officer did something wrong. Why else would he feel the need to organize a race committee? According to the police report and other officers at the scene (one of which was black), Officer Crowley performed his duty by the book.

Obama's refusal to apologize to America's police sends a horrible message to black America. Speaking from the highest office in the land, his words give tremendous credence to the "blacks are victims" paradigm. Think of the hatred and resentment Obama's false assumption that police typically mistreat blacks will inspire in black youths. My goodness, the President of the United States agrees with the gangster rappers, "Yo, if you're black in A-mur-a-ka, da Man is out ta getcha."

Remember the controversy and fear of violence because of the rap song, "Cop Killer" by Ice-T? Our president's comments were extremely divisive and irresponsible.

Something else disturbs me regarding Obama's handling of the Gates/ Crowley incident. Obama could have simply apologized to police for calling them stupid, and America would have moved on. Instead, he chose to organize a race committee and invite Gates and Officer Crowley, to the White House for a beer. So rather than admitting that he misspoke, in essence, Obama threw America's police and their relationship with the black community under the bus to save face.

This is not the behavior of a "Great Unifier" Obama voters thought they were electing. Sadly, it is the behavior of a selfish, ego-driven small man.

Just as O.J. Simpson's attorneys masterfully turned his trial from being about a husband decapitating his wife to reparations for the persecution of blacks in America, the Gates case morphed from an arrest for disorderly conduct to a White House study on racial profiling and police mistreatment of blacks.

Following the "Beer Summit" Democrats launched "Operation Defend Obama" at all costs. TV programs were littered with Democrats, race profiteers and bitter racists defending Obama's statement. Their mantra, "Cops do abuse blacks" sounded like it was 1959 rather than 2009.

This is nothing new in the liberal playbook. To save their own, Democrats are notorious for sacrificing anyone and everyone. Democratic President Bill Clinton had oral sex with an intern in the Oval Office. To defend Clinton, Democrats impugned the integrity and character of all men. Every Clinton administration spokesperson and liberal media person implied that any man, if given the opportunity, would have reacted like Clinton. Think about that folks: according to their spin, your pastor, father, grandfather, husband, soccer coach, school teacher and doctor would display the same lack of restraint and character as Clinton if "hit on" by a young woman.

Democrats did the same when the Speaker of the House Nancy Pelosi, without evidence, accused the CIA of lying. Did the Democrats encourage Pelosi to apologize for challenging the credibility of this organization so vital to our national security? No. Instead, they set out to trash the CIA and throw it under the bus.

During the Bush years, Democrats resembled Captain Ahab in the novel *Moby Dick*. In their obsession to kill their white whale, George W. Bush, they attacked our military. Shamefully, Democrats accused the brave young men and women who volunteered to defend us, some even paying the ultimate sacrifice, of being rapists and murderers, throwing them under the bus.

With our troops on the battle field in Iraq, Democrat Senator Harry Reid announced to the world that the war was lost. Can you imagine the damage Reid's statement did to the morale of our troops? When decorated General Petraeus reported the war had turned in our favor, Democrats disgracefully called him a liar. Blinded by their obsession to "get Bush," putting the lives of our troops at risk was merely collateral damage to the Democrats. I take the attacks on our military very seriously.

Remember the book, *Everything I Needed to Know I Learned in Kindergarten*? Everything I needed to know about war and combat I learned in elementary school. Sometimes war is necessary and even honorable. And thank God for men who are gifted in the art of war.

My cousin, Jimmy, and I went to the same Baltimore city elementary school until I was in fifth grade when my family moved to the suburbs. Jimmy's family was on welfare. His mom (my mom's sister), had five boys by three different men. Neither of the men supported or visited their sons. Jimmy was wild, tough and fearless. He had a very short fuse and a well earned reputation as a fighter. I was a small sensitive kid.

As cliche-ish as this sounds, two bullies were beating me up and taking my lunch money. I told Jimmy. He immediately confronted them, put them on the defensive, and my problem was over. Word spread through the schoolyard grapevine that I was Jimmy's cousin and not to be messed with. Jimmy's ability to fight and his willingness to go to war did for me what I could not do for myself. I am thankful and grateful for Jimmy.

In 2007, I was truly offended when a Florida elementary school teacher planned to put the names of conscientious objectors on a banner at a Veterans Day observance. The teacher wanted to honor conscientious objectors and give them what was described as more or less equal recognition with veterans.

On Veterans Day, a television program featured a conscientious objector. The program portrayed him as supremely enlightened. It was sickening. I kept thinking that thanks to the sacrifice, blood, sweat and tears of brave fighting men and women, the guy is free to pontificate about how he finds violence distasteful.

Peaceniks do not understand that bullies are bullies whether in the schoolyard or in the world arena. Nice words do not affect these megalomaniacs. They view your attempts to reason with them as a weakness to be exploited. Their self-centered mindsets only understand self-preservation. Our brave honorable fighting men and women deserve our highest respect and gratitude. May God continue to bless and preserve our military.

Every Democrat decision is always about preserving and gaining power. We Americans do not want race-based law enforcement. Nor do we want Supreme Court justices overruling the Constitution with their feelings. Nor do we want the brave men and women serving in our military, CIA and law enforcement used as political pawns. We The People demand adherence to the Constitution and equal justice for all, plain and simple.

Lloyd with a Tea Party Participant
Washington, DC 9-12-09

Chapter 12

Getting the Truth Out to Black America

While flipping through the TV channels with my remote, I stopped on the movie, *Diary of a Mad Black Woman* on BET (Black Entertainment Television), which is an excellent movie. During a commercial break, they gave a news update. An announcer said, "They tried to get the Bronx kid, Sonia Sotomayor, but she beat them." There was not one mention of Sotomayor's controversial racist statements. Thus, black viewers who don't follow the news closely are led to conclude that those "evil racist white Republicans" are at it again, trying to block a person of color. Urban radio is also guilty of unfair and unbalanced liberal reporting.

I wonder how BET reported the Democrats' trashing of black Supreme Court Justices Clarence Thomas and Hispanic Alberto Gonzalez? It probably went something like this:

"Well, those two traitors deserved to be trashed. How dare they prosper without Affirmative Action and lowered standards which contradict the premise of victimhood championed by Democrats, education, hard work and character? Heck No! We cannot allow such a conservative message to influence black youths. These Uncle Toms must be destroyed!"

The announcer went on to praise Obama for his Surgeon General nominee, Regina Benjamin, a black woman. Again, no mention of Benjamin's politics, which are far left. The report glowingly praised Benjamin for her wonderful work helping victims of hurricane Katrina. Any opposition to Benjamin will surely be reported as more racism from those freaking SOB Republicans.

This is a huge disservice to African-Americans. No wonder Obama received 96% of the black vote. No wonder Black Americans do not have a clue regarding what is truly going on in our country. All they are fed is "Obama good. White racist Republicans bad." Why does black media continue giving aid and comfort to the real enemies of minority progress?

With the majority of black Americans getting their news from black and white liberal media, there is very little chance of them hearing the truth. Fortunately, I escaped the liberal plantation in the early 90s when I was exposed to Rush Limbaugh. Listening to Rush introduced me to brilliant black conservatives like Thomas Sowell and Walter E. Williams.

I thought, *Why haven't these guys been featured on Oprah or honored at the NAACP awards?*

Answer: These blacks are paradigm breakers. They do not fit the "we are black, thus special concessions must be made for us" template.

How do we get the truth to black America? There are numerous modestly funded conservative black organizations; Project 21, NBRA.info and CURE to name a few. Recently, RagingElephants.Org drove liberals crazy with their "MLK was a Republican" billboard. I loved it! We need much, much more bold, in your face messages like this. These courageous black patriots need your support.

Emancipation. Revelation. Revolution. won Best Cutting Edge Film at the NOIR Film festival in 2006. The documentary chronicles the civil rights movement in America and the role that both major political parties played in it. This extremely revealing and educating film has yet to receive major exposure (ERRvideo.com).

I am President of the NAACPC, National Association for the Advancement of Conservative People of Color. At first, I rejected the position for the same reasons I rejected joining a Black Republican Club. I thought, "We are all Americans with the same concerns and desires for our country and families."

Why is a black group necessary? I still do not personally feel the need to belong to a Black Republican Club, but to Republican blacks who do, fine. All efforts to set blacks free have my full support.

However, my NAACPC is about educating, not just black America, but all Americans to the truth that conservatism is the most direct and fulfilling route to achieving the American Dream.

There are incidents in the Bible when God removed the scales from the eyes of individuals enabling them to see and receive the truth. This is my prayer for a black America blinded by liberalism.

Lloyd Marcus & Katrina Pierson
Tea Party Speaker in Dallas, TX

Chapter 13

Trusting God and Not Government

I s God back? While watching the Glenn Beck pro gram, three women-yes, I said three-boldly proclaimed their Christianity and how their decision to follow Christ has affected their politics. Other than religious programs, people do not talk about their faith on TV without being portrayed as fanatics or nut cases. It was truly refreshing. Could this mean God is back from exile from the public square?

Tragically, many look to government, their boss, or someone as their source. I have learned that God is my only source. With this knowledge comes great liberation. I do not need to work hard to be liked, or force friendships or kiss butt to get promoted. I simply treat people with love and respect, keep my word and do my job to the best of my ability. In His timing, God continues to promote me.

After Mary and I relocated from Maryland to Florida for the job offer of a lifetime, the offer fell through. In all honesty, there was nothing back in Maryland for us, so we decided to stay in Florida. To say that starting over and establishing ourselves in a new state was difficult would be an understatement. Many times it was scary and emotionally painful. Time after time we were brought to the edge of ruin and catastrophe only to be miraculously delivered. Our spiritual journey has been full of highs and lows. But the lowest point occurred while Mary and I were homeless.

We mistakenly trusted an incompetent mortgage broker. Following her instructions, we gave our landlord a thirty day notice that we were moving out of the house we were renting. Instantly, our landlord found new tenants. At the end of thirty days, our deal fell through for the new house. I realized we could have probably gone to court and won legal rights to stay in the rental, but I had given my word. Causing our landlord grief and complicating the lives of others just didn't seem right.

Mary and I had no place to go. On our final day in the rental, Mary made several phone calls trying to find shelter. We expected God to ride in on a white horse and save the day just as He had done so many times in the past. This time, He did not. With the help of a friend named Frank and his family, we moved out of the rental in one day. Mary and I were faced with a shocking reality. We were homeless.

This was an unbelievable contrast to who we had been most of our lives. For 15 years I was a highly successful award winning graphic designer at a major market television station in Maryland. My television singing appearances and community work made me somewhat of a celebrity. We owned a beautiful home with a swimming pool, had two cars and dined in expensive restaurants a few times a week. We were often featured in the society pages, many times for our annual "Lloyd & Mary's Island Party."

A few months before becoming homeless, I accepted the nonpaid position of President of the Deltona Arts & Historical Center. The offer came as a result of my high profile involvement in arts projects in the community. We desperately needed money. I asked Mary, "Why on earth should I take on a nonpaid position?" She replied, "I just think you should do it." As President, I had a door key. Mary and I could see no other option than to secretly move into the arts center.

Our mortgage broker from hell assured us that she would patch up our deal and get us into our new home in a couple of weeks. Everything we could not fit into storage, we hid at the arts center including our two dogs, cat and two birds. The center was open to the public on weekdays. Mary and I would pretend to go home at day's end and sneak back later. We slept on a blow up mattress. Every night, I parked my car a block away and walked back to the center so our car would not be seen at the center all night. The founder of the center also had a key. We lived with the fear of being humiliated by him unexpectedly walking in on us.

Homelessness put us in a Catch 22 situation. We were struggling to acquire singing gigs for me and being displaced made it all the more difficult. We hid at the arts center for six months before miraculously landing a home with a rent to own option.

Because we thought we would only be homeless for two weeks, we stored our clothes in the back of the storage unit. To get to our clothes we would have to remove all of our furniture. Consequently, Mary and I purchased a few items from a thrift store and wore them for six months. The lack of privacy, security and stress of hiding was taking its toll on Mary.

Though we prayed faithfully and tried everything to move forward, nothing seemed to be changing. It's funny how sometimes when you are in the wilderness, God doesn't remove you. Instead, He gives you a cool drink of water to keep you going. God's cool drink came to us in the form of a week of house sitting for a friend vacationing out of the country. Another refreshing break came from our dear friends Bob and Camille. They invited us to spend an all expense paid weekend with them in Las Vegas. Those two escapes were perfectly timed, extremely needed and greatly appreciated.

One night at the art center, while I was blowing up the air mattress, I heard Mary scream like I had never heard in our twenty-five years of marriage. She had broken her front tooth while eating a candy bar. Mary's long soul stirring sobs and river of tears came from a place deep within her. Feeling helpless, all I could do was hold her. It was as if this incident epitomized everything that had gone wrong since we moved to Florida. It was the straw that broke the camel's back. We were homeless, driving a horrible old van with a broken windshield, financially broke and now even her smile was gone.

I vowed to get her tooth repaired. While I would never break the law, I chuckled to myself at the thought of me robbing our local convenience store. I have a lifelong stutter in my speech. I imagined pointing my finger under my shirt at the clerk and saying, "Give me the m-m-money!" and the clerk saying, "Lloyd, is that you under that hood?"

That night was the lowest of our lives. The following day, a friend got his dentist to repair Mary's tooth on credit.

Looking back at our homeless experience, it bonded us to the arts center which became the foundation of our extraordinary success. The ordeal changed us in ways we still to do not fully comprehend. We are stronger and appreciate all that God has given us.

We were once spoiled and arrogant trusting only in our smarts, knowledge and self-reliance. In the Bible Jesus said, "Without Me, you can do nothing." Mary and I have learned this to be true. Today, we only trust God.

My experience with others also taught me that sometimes your dreams are fulfilled through helping others to pursue their dreams. It is crucial that you are lead by the Holy Spirit. If not, some folks will use and abuse you. God gives us His grace for people and situations where He wants us. Do not allow yourself to be made to feel guilty and manipulated by others. God's leading is a personal thing.

For example, friends were collecting $10 per person for a girl in need. My wife and I did not feel good about giving to the cause. We thought, *This is ridiculous, they are only asking for ten bucks.* Still, we did not feel good about giving. And yet, on another occasion, we borrowed funds from a finance company to help a couple in need. It does not take a financial genius to know it is not good business to borrow money only to give it away. Mary and I had total peace about it. Our gesture sparked an extremely bonding friendship with that couple which we cherish to this day. They have paid us back in funds, services and friendship far beyond our original gift to them.

I am not encouraging making ignorant business decisions. Nor am I encouraging having a hard heart to those in need. I am saying to be led by God and realize it is not always about you. My experience with DC taught me this.

After quitting my job to pursue a music career, Mary and I had fallen six months behind in our mortgage. I teamed up with a deejay to form "The Party Guys." Bob, my deejay partner spun records and I sang some songs to karaoke tracks and worked the crowd. We did a great job, but the gigs were not steady. I also hit the bricks seeking freelance graphic design jobs. Still, nothing was working and Mary and I struggled for food and gas money.

Our neighbor was an elderly retired black gentleman named DC. His adult niece lived with him. She worked and DC was alone all day with the exception of the time he spent at kidney dialysis every other day. Walking was difficult for him. One day, he asked me to help him with a project. I can't remember what the project was, but it was the first of many. I became his "Man Friday." I drove him to appointments, did landscaping for him, and helped him plant his small vegetable garden. More accurately, I dug, tilled the soil, fertilized and planted while DC supervised.

DC had a horrible childhood. He was a hard man with only a sixth grade education. Still, he was a somewhat successful businessman, owning two homes and three vehicles. DC had a list of folks he hated. While he respected me as a man of faith, talking about God or forgiveness made him angry.

Our relationship was symbiotic. DC needed my physical abilities and companionship. Helping him kept my mind off of myself and my financial woes. We enjoyed each other's company.

On one of my weekly visits, I knocked, walked in and found DC sitting silent in his favorite chair. I said my usual cheerful hello, but he said nothing. I walked up behind him. When I placed my hand on his shoulder, DC began to quietly cry. His tears of pain grew deeper, louder and lasted for several minutes. Without comment, I patted his shoulders.

Though we never discussed his emotional breakdown, I felt like a dam of hurt and pain was released from him that day. A month or so later, DC's diabetes took a turn for the worse. When his niece told me that the ambulance had taken him to the hospital, I rushed to see him. DC couldn't speak, but I know he knew I was there. I held his hand and quietly sang to him. I sang "Amazing Grace" and "What A Friend

We Have in Jesus." When I left, I felt a sense of peace about him. At four o'clock in the morning, DC died. I believe with all my heart DC made his peace with God.

My mom passed away in 1992 just before I quit my job at the television station. A child of the Depression, she would have never approved of me throwing away my secure dream job to pursue a crazy dream of a music career. During the time I was helping DC, I had a dream about my mom. In my dream Mom said, "I've thought about it and you do not have to go back to the television station."

The next day after Mom visited me in a dream, I received a call back on a freelance graphic design job. Once I started helping DC and stopped focusing on myself and my problems, other doors began opening.

Lloyd and Mary Marcus Whitehouse Christmas

While we may not know it at the time, God has plans for each of us. God had a plan bringing Mary and I, two wild and crazy kids. Despite all of my flaws, Mary still thinks I'm the best thing since sliced bread, and brings me coffee in bed every morning. She has been the perfect helpmeet for me to fulfill God's purpose for my life. I can honestly say, I would not be touching the lives of millions through my music and writings if it were not for Mary.

Chapter 14

Married to a White Woman

In 1973, while walking from my townhouse apartment to the parking lot, a young, blonde, white female neighbor solicited my assistance. She had locked herself out of her apartment. Mary asked me to climb through her window. Perhaps I should have been offended by her assuming that I, a black guy, was skilled in breaking into apartments. I broke in and we laughed and talked for several hours.

At the time I was in an extremely unhappy marriage. My wife, Barbara, and I married for the wrong reasons and had different plans for our lives. You would think we would have discussed such things before tying the knot. Consequently, we said and did very painful things to each other. As I chatted with Mary, it occurred to me that in our entire five years of marriage, my wife and I had never sat laughing and talking. The one good thing that came out of our marriage was my daughter, Lisa, who was born in 1971.

Mary was a single mom with a son. She had recently divorced, her relationship with her ex also a casualty of opposing life agendas. Because her parents sided with her ex, he won custody of her son. It was not long before Mary and I became an item, and after many heated arguments, Barbara took Lisa and moved out. A few days later, Mary moved in.

Mary and I were young, wild and irresponsible. Though we both kept jobs, we used marijuana and alcohol excessively. We did the nightclub scene several nights a week. This behavior went on for a fews years.

Early in our dating, I caught Mary crying in the bedroom. She said she had a vision of us being together for a very long time. At that time, shortly after separating from my wife, I thought Mary was just a rest stop.

I grew weary of my debauchery. In my bedroom, I asked Jesus to help me. Suddenly, I felt an overwhelming sense of love and relief. With tears rolling down my face, I joyously told Mary of my miraculous experience. I flushed a substantial amount of marijuana down the toilet, but Mary was not convinced and kept her small stash. I began reading the Bible and regularly attending church. Still not convinced, Mary investigated to confirm that I was attending church and not secretly dating. The real confirmation of my spiritual conversion came when I announced that I would no longer be intimate with her without marriage. Eventually, Mary also made a spiritual life-style change.

We married in a state park. Our guests paid one dollar a carload to enter and brought covered dishes. Both our families refused to attend with the exception of my middle brother, Jerry. He agreed to be my best man, but got lost and came after the ceremony. I asked a guest to stand in for him as best man.

Beginning our interracial love affair in the early 70s, we survived hatred from both sides. We were threatened, chased in our car, assaulted in a restaurant with a beer bottle, and endured angry comments from strangers. In the early years, we were rejected by family and friends. Still, Mary has never wavered in her love and commitment to me.

From the first night I met her, Mary said she saw greatness in me. After thirty years of marriage, her perception of me has not changed. Graciously, it has increased. Early in our relationship people sensed a powerful bond between Mary and me which continues today. I am eternally grateful and thankful to God for her. I am bountifully blessed. Despite the failure of my marriage to Lisa's mom, God still had a purpose for our union. For one thing, it produced Lisa. And for that, I am eternally grateful.

In 1970, upon flunking out of art college (too much partying), I was immediately drafted into the U.S. Army. Uncle Sam bused me from Baltimore, MD to Fort Bragg, NC for boot camp. For most of us young recruits, it was our first time away from home. Everything stopped when we heard, "Mail call!" Guys would come running, half naked if they were in the shower. Anything from home was exciting, even a newspaper.

I was a newlywed. My prom date, Barbara, and I married a month before I had to report for duty. The day she visited me at boot camp was the first I had seen her in six weeks or more. We had a great dinner and got trashed on several rounds of a popular new drink called a "Hurricane." We retired to one of the cabins on the Army base provided for married couples. We enjoyed a lovemaking marathon.

A month or so later in the barracks, someone yelled, "Marcus...phone!" Wrapped in only a towel, I ran down the long hall from my room to the wall phone. It was Barbara calling from Baltimore. She said she was pregnant. I jumped up and down with excitement. I was overjoyed.

After boot camp, I was stationed at Fort Bragg for my entire two years in the Army. This can only by explained as divine intervention. Our battalion was a little over 500 troops. Upon returning from a short leave, the buzz was that everyone had orders for Vietnam. My name along with two or three other guys was not on the list. To this day, I do not know how or why that happened.

I was an illustrator in the Psychological Warfare Department in the morning, and rehearsed with the Green Beret Chorus in the afternoon. I found a charming log cabin style cottage off base and moved my pregnant wife down from Baltimore. The property owner was quite frank. "I normally don't rent to coloreds, but I'll rent to you." I guess there's a compliment in there somewhere.

One December day, my wife said, "I think it's time." Nervous and excited, I loaded her into the car and headed for the hospital. Our car broke down en route. Since this was before cell phones, our only option was to start hitch-hiking. I held Barbara's hand and stuck out my thumb with the other. A stereotypical bright colored hand-painted hippie Volkswagen van pulled over. It was full of young, white hippies. A cloud of marijuana smoke escaped when they opened the door. They were excited and eager to give us a ride to the hospital. And yes, I did accept their gracious offer to indulge in a few tokes of cannabis.

At the hospital, a nurse took Barbara and returned a while later. She handed me a brown paper bag. Inside was Barbara's clothes. Perhaps it was the emotion of everything that was happening or a side effect of the cannabis, I looked at the bag and unexpectedly cried. I hitchhiked home.

The next morning I received a call, "Mr. Marcus, it's a girl!" Lisa Maria Marcus was born December 17, 1971. I was honorably discharged after two years. Barbara and I moved back home to Maryland. We found an affordable apartment in a Baltimore suburb. My beautiful daughter, Lisa, would be the only good thing to come out of our five years of marriage.

Marriage counseling revealed that we married too young and for the wrong reasons. Barbara married me to get away from home. I always felt she was not fully committed to me, but her admission broke my heart. My reason for tying the knot was equally shallow. I married Barbara because she was the prettiest girl in the choir. It never dawned on either of us that a lifelong commitment such as marriage requires much more in common. We had opposing philosophies and desired directions for our lives. Consequently, we feuded about everything and hurt each other deeply. Our marriage ended with me screaming at Barbara in a painful drunken rage. She took Lisa and left.

Over time, I grew weary of my "road to nowhere" life. I asked Jesus to help me and He did. Even though Mary and I had been living together for a few years, I felt obligated to attempt to restore my marriage with Barbara. My attempt failed.

Our divorce cost me fifty bucks. After hearing the final decree that Barbara and I were no longer married, I closed myself into one of the stalls in the courthouse restroom and wept deeply. I felt like an amputee, like a part of my body was cut away. I couldn't explain my feelings. I no longer wanted to be married to Barbara. So why was I in so much pain?

Long distance fatherhood is hard. Barbara was pretty reasonable about allowing me to see Lisa. Over the years, Lisa and I have had good times together. I loved the time she threw a perfect strike from center field getting a runner out at home plate during a company picnic. She laughs about the time I did a belly flop off the diving board. "Dad, I didn't think there would be any water left in the pool after that one." However, I've never had an active role in her life. Overcoming the guilt remains a challenge.

Lisa entered the U.S. Navy after graduating high school. She has worked her way up through the ranks to become an officer. She is beautiful, extremely bright, honorable and a born leader. If I sound like a proud dad, I am.

Lloyd is a Great American!

Chapter 15

Sarah Palin at High Noon

I just watched the classic movie, *High Noon* (again). Gary Cooper played a brave sheriff who brought law and order to his town. As one woman said, "He made it safe for a decent woman to walk down the street."

A recently released outlaw was coming back to town on the noon train to deliver vengeance against the sheriff who put him away. His gang of three arrived early to help their leader take out the sheriff.

Fully aware of why the bad men were in town, the sheriff could not arrest them because they had not broken any laws. Waiting is not illegal.

Desperate, the sheriff interrupted a church service to solicit help. After much debate, the ungrateful town folks declined. They even suggested the sheriff "get out of town" hoping the trouble would follow him. The sheriff contemplated their recommendation. He began saddling his horse, but something inside him would not allow him to run away. Heroically, the sheriff faced the bad guys and won.

I thought of another strong, gutsy, bold, and stand-on-principles hero, Sarah Palin, in her own modern day version of "High Noon." Sheriff Palin rode into America Town on a white horse with conservative guns blazing and saved a dead McCain campaign. She brought hope to weary and battered conservative town folks and gave them a reason to vote.

Outlaw Obama and his posse, the hate filled liberal media/Democrat gang, came to town a gunnin' to politically eliminate Sheriff Palin. They ambushed her at Miss Katie Couric's CBS saloon. Though wounded numerous times, Sheriff Palin survived.

She bravely stood tall and rode high in the saddle while ungrateful, weak-kneed Republican town folks ran for cover, hid in their homes, and nervously peeked through the curtains.

Why are Obama and his gang so committed and desperate to destroy Palin? Could it be they recognize her destiny, like that of Moses, to set her people free? Why is she so despised by them? Obama's gang hate Palin for all the reasons we love her. Sheriff Palin is a good, decent, and strong character-driven conservative leader. Palin also believes in God. Such humility and virtues are as repulsive to liberals as showing Dracula the cross.

What sticks in the craw of many liberal women is that in their youth, they bought into the feminist rhetoric that women's liberation means no husband and family. Tragically, they find themselves aging and alone. Meanwhile, this conservative woman has it all: great career, fine family and a husband who loves and respects her. Adding insult in injury, Sheriff Palin looks mighty fine in her jeans.

Recently, the libs sent an old washed up gunslinger, the Letterman Kid, to challenge Sheriff Palin to a shoot-out. Palin planted two bullets between the pathetic old dude's wrinkly eyes before he could un-holster his gun.

Despite Sheriff Palin's courage and willingness to fight, Obama and his posse rule America Town. They are in the process of taking over everything! Obama took over the livery stable and banned horses. While he and his posse continue riding horses, we town folks are forced to ride miniature ponies.

But in the spirit of what has made America Town great, an uprising is a brewin', with a huge conservative posse building daily. Our first battle will be in 2010 to win back America Town's House and Senate. Then, in 2012, God willing and the creek don't rise, Sheriff Palin will lead us to victory in the battle of Little Big Washington, DC. Years earlier, another great lawman cleaned up America Town. His name was Ronald Reagan.

After Sheriff Palin sweeps out the Obama gang, perhaps once again, we will be as what Sheriff Reagan affectionately called us, "a shining city on a hill."

The CD Cover photo for American Tea Party Anthem

Conclusion

I pray that I have encouraged and inspired you. We have much to do to restore and maintain our freedom, liberty and culture. I also long to see the day when my fellow blacks will no longer suffer the indignity, slavery and detriment to their self-esteem which comes through having a victim mindset instilled by liberals. Dr. King dreamed of a day when people (black and white) would be judged by the content of their character rather than the color of their skin. I share his dream.

Though the enemies of freedom and true brotherhood appear so large and overwhelmingly powerful, I take great comfort in knowing, "The battle is not ours, it is the Lord's." All is well. Go in peace and live a great life!

Love,

Lloyd

Finally, Your Wait is Over!

$15.95 (plus S/H)

Online at www.itouchpublishers.com
or call 24/7
800-791-5806 ext. 150

A great fund raiser for your grassroots organization.
Request discount rates for various quantities.

The 12 Great Songs

1. American Tea Party Anthem

2. We The People

3 Feet to the Fire

4 Wonderful Country

5. Twenty -Ten (performed live for a million plus patriots at 912 DC rally)

6. Our Girls (a tribute to Sarah Palin, Ann Coulter, Laura Ingraham & Michelle Malkin)
7. Hello Mom, it's Me (pro-life song, based on a true story)
8. Let the River Flow
9. United We Stand
10. Can't Afford the Sunshine
11. Dance with the Devil
12 It's About Love

Dear Patriots,
Please support my efforts to serve our peerless country by purchasing my new CD.

I'm an Unhyphenated American who believes as President Ronald Reagan that:

"America is a shining city on a hill."

The radical changes planned by the Obama administration are an abomination of the divinely inspired vision of our Founding Fathers.

We MUST, and we Will, Take Back America!

www.lloydmarcus.com

www.higherstandardpublishers.com
Order By Phone: 800-791-5806 ext. 150

Other outstanding books by
Higher Standard Publishers

Help! Mom! Radicals Are Ruining My Country
by Katharine Debrecht

From the author of the bestselling, Help! Mom! There Are Liberals Under My Bed! Katharine DeBrecht, comes Help! Mom! Radicals Are Ruining My Country! - a hilarious and entertaining way for parents to sit down with their children and teach them the origins of the new Tea Party movement and the importance of standing up for liberty and the American Dream.

64 pages with illustrations ISBN: 0-9824027-8-3 $19.95

The Power Within a Conservative Woman
by Selena Owens

Many powerful conservative women have gone before us as examples of courage and leadership. Through their undying support and belief in God; of the Founders' thoughtful decision to break with Britain; and of their own inspiration to live in a land free from tyranny and oppression, these model women fought for the very same ideals that we are fighting for today

96 pages / ISBN: 0-9824027-5-9 $9.95

Obama: Why Black America Should Have Doubts
by William Owens

The purpose of this book is to challenge us all as Americans to look deeper at Barack Obama the man, his voting record, and his position on the important issues facing our country. I urge you, don't put your race before your principles, before the truth, before your family, and before your own country.

146 pages ./ ISBN - 978-1-60702-073-8 $16.95

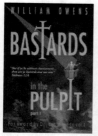

Bastards in the Pulpit! - Part 1
By William Owens

Bastards in the Pulpit is certainly not about faith that demands God to do something new for you. It is not about how to conduct a successful conference. It has nothing to do with being popular among people. It is far from man's idea of positive. To many, it will appear to be in error and perhaps from the pit of hell. For those who use His grace to practice lasciviousness, you certainly will be appalled. Then again, perhaps the Spirit of the Lord will have mercy and allow you to see the soulishness of your heart. *Bastards in the Pulpit* is not written to sell a million but to please one: God!   140 pages / ISBN: 0-9658629-0-9 $14.95

Divine Protocol
The Order of God's Kingdom By William Owens

From our families at home to our fellowship at our churches, God is demanding Divine Protocol: The Order of God's Kingdom. Away with the traditions and commandments of men that are comprised of opinions, prejudices, and sins ranging from willful sin, racism, unforgiveness toward one another, and contempt toward the Holy Ghost. May we now embark upon a glimpse of God's order, God's plan, God's way, known as Divine Protocol.   **240 Pages / ISBN: 0-9-658629-9-2** $21.95

Helpmeet: *The Power to*
Help Your Husband By Selena Owens

Learn the wisdom of how a wife helps her husband the way God has ordained and decreed. This is an inspired message about fearing God and keeping His commandments, loving your husband as unto the Lord, submitting to the appointed authority in your home, and lastly, preparing your heart to be a helpmeet to your husband. Be ready to receive the word of the Lord as it applies to you and your situation and above all else, seek the Lord on effectively producing godly fruit.
140 pages / **ISBN 0-9658629-1-7** $11.95

Warriors Arise! By William Owens
Spiritual Life • Spiritual Maturity • Spiritual Warfare

Ephesians 6:12 For we wrestle not against flesh and blood, but against principalities, against powers, against the rulers of the darkness of this world, against spiritual wickedness in high places.

There is a clarion call for those who would be perfected and attend to the spiritual realm of God's kingdom. As God's kingdom unfolds in these last days, it's imperative that the Church answer the call of spiritual warfare.
128 pages $9.95

Higher Standard Publishers
www.higherstandardpublishers.com
Order By Phone: 800-791-5806 ext. 150